REDISCOVERING
the
BOOK
of
REVELATION

BARCLAY M. NEWMAN, JR.

Rediscovering
the
Book
of
Revelation

THE JUDSON PRESS
VALLEY FORGE

REDISCOVERING
THE
BOOK
OF
REVELATION

49, 196

To the memory of my mother and stepfather
Lillie Mae
and
Reyburn H. Frey

contents

Introduction

RECENT STUDIES HAVE CAST A MUCH-NEEDED LIGHT ON THE
ancient gnostic heresies, which through a multiplicity of
expressions competed with the message of the early church.
Through the results of these studies, interpreters now are
able to understand more adequately many hitherto dark
passages in the New Testament.

For example, it has long been recognized that the problems of immorality and idolatry reflected in Revelation 2-3
represent problems produced by the adoption of the gnostic
libertine attitude on the part of some who professed to be
Christian disciples; but as yet no one has related these
passages to the possibility that Revelation in its *entirety*
was written against the background of conflict with this
libertine gnostic movement. The intention of this volume
is, therefore, to set forth the theory that the book of Revelation was written primarily to refute the teachings and
influence of a gnostic group which had entered the churches
of Asia Minor under the guise of a more perfect form of
Christianity.

The style of this book is such that layman and minister
alike should find it easy to read; and, regardless of one's
previous orientation to the book of Revelation, it is hoped
that all readers will find the presentation in this volume
to be both provocative and stimulating. The first three

chapters, brief in relation to the one that follows, lay the foundation for the exposition of Revelation contained in Chapter 4. A final chapter brings together the results of the study and points out some of the values of Revelation for the present life of the church.

Quotations from Irenaeus and Hippolytus are from Volumes I and V of *The Ante-Nicene Fathers,* edited by Alexander Roberts and James Donaldson, and are used by permission of Wm. B. Eerdmans Publishing Company, Grand Rapids, Michigan.

Although the material of the book is in a quite different form, the conclusions herein reached are based in part upon the research done in conjunction with my Th. D. dissertation entitled "A Consideration of the Apocalypse as an Anti-Gnostic Document" at the Southern Baptist Theological Seminary, Louisville, Kentucky, 1960. The first chapter of this book represents a reworking of my article "The Fallacy of the Domitian Hypothesis: Critique of the Irenaeus Source as a Witness for the Contemporary-historical Approach to the Interpretation of the Apocalypse," which appeared in *New Testament Studies,* Volume 10, 1963. Special appreciation is given to Dr. Glenn Hinson of the Southern Baptist Theological Seminary in Louisville, Kentucky, for his careful checking of the footnotes and bibliographical references.

BARCLAY M. NEWMAN, JR.

the Route
that
Leads
to
Rediscovery[1]

Among present-day New Testament scholars it is almost unanimously agreed that the book of Revelation was written at a period late in the first century, when the churches of Asia Minor were undergoing persecution by the Roman authorities.[2] Furthermore, in keeping with that basic viewpoint, it is held that the mysterious symbols used by the author, especially those of Chapters 13 and 17, reflect certain aspects of this persecution. As a rule, the figure of Babylon (17:1-18) is believed to symbolize Rome; the first beast (13:1-10), the emperor cult; the second beast (13:11-18), its priesthood; and the seven heads of the first beast (13:1), Roman emperors, among whom is Nero. So generally accepted and unquestioned is this view that one of its recent representatives can affirm:

> It is obvious that Revelation was written in a time when the Christians of Asia Minor, and probably other places as well, were being persecuted by the Roman officials for their refusal to worship the emperors. . . .[3]

Basic presuppositions of the present route. This method of interpreting the book of Revelation, known as the contemporary-historical approach, is based primarily on a two-fold assumption. First, since Revelation is written in apocalyptic symbolism, it is assumed that the book reflects a background of political-religious persecution like most of

11

the Jewish apocalypses which preceded it. Second, according to the most reliable early testimony it was composed during the reign of the emperor Domitian (A.D. 81-96). By combining these two presuppositions, the proponents of this view conclude that Revelation reflects a persecution of the early church by the emperor Domitian.

But one must not assume that the book of Revelation reflects the background of a political-religious persecution merely because several of the earlier Jewish apocalypses appear to have been written at a time when the Jewish nation was undergoing persecution for its faith. Similarity of *form* to these earlier apocalypses does not necessarily indicate similarity of *background*. Indeed, Revelation differs in several significant ways from the earlier Jewish apocalypses. Revelation is more than a link in a chain; and it must not be looked upon as the repeated product of an ancient tradition. Rather it must be regarded as a unique product of literature, to be understood only in light of the meaning given by the author himself.

In order to determine what the seer intended by the symbols he used, *one must remain within the context of Revelation itself*. For example, a kindred relationship exists between apocalyptic literature and Dante's *The Divine Comedy*, yet no one attempts to interpret Dante against a background similar to that of the literature from which he drew his imagery. So it is that factors other than those pertaining to a political-religious persecution could easily have been the common denominator between Revelation and other apocalyptic literature.[4]

An essential element in all apocalyptic literature, both Jewish and Christian, is the revelation of a special knowledge (better known by its technical name, *gnosis*)[5] to the elect, by which is made known to them the secret mysteries of redemption. Through the assistance of the Spirit the initiated are enabled to know and speak what was hitherto hidden. Thus the possibility exists that a *gnosis* motif may be the determinative factor, both in the purpose and in the construction of Revelation. Since, among the early witnesses to Revelation, Irenaeus is the most important in this regard, it will be fruitful to examine briefly what he has to say.

Irenaeus dates the writing of Revelation in the last part of Domitian's reign: "For that [the apocalyptic vision] was seen no very long time since, but almost in our day, towards the end of Domitian's reign" (Irenaeus *Against Heresies* V. xxx. 3). Aided by this information, the proponents of the contemporary-historical approach attempt to make certain vague allusions in Revelation conform to their concept of what the supposed persecution of the church by Domitian must have meant to the church.[6]

However, and this is important to notice, Irenaeus does *not* state that Revelation reflects a persecution of the church under Domitian, only that it is to be *dated* during his reign. If one reads closely, it will be noted that Irenaeus himself renders an allegorical interpretation of Revelation. And, furthermore, he uses Revelation in this manner to describe the fate of the apostates in all generations since the beginning of the world, with particular reference to those of his own generation who were committing *apostasy to gnosticism.*

In a still clearer light has John, in the Apocalypse, indicated to the Lord's disciples what shall happen in the last times, and concerning the ten kings who shall then arise, among whom the empire which now rules [the earth] shall be partitioned. . . . Let those persons, therefore, who blaspheme the Creator, either by openly expressed words, such as the disciples of Marcion, or by a perversion of the sense [of Scripture], as those of Valentinus and all the Gnostics falsely so called, be recognised as agents of Satan by all those who worship God; through whose agency Satan now, and not before, has been seen to speak against God, even Him who has prepared eternal fire for every kind of apostasy (Irenaeus *Against Heresies* V. xxvi. 1).

Where Irenaeus makes reference to speculations concerning the number 666 (Revelation 13:18), he does so to refute any mistaken notion that this number should be interpreted in light of the succession of Roman emperors. In no instance does he even hint that he is familiar with the theory that the number reflects a belief in the return to life and power of Nero. As the editors of the Ante-Nicene edition remark at this passage, ". . . let us imitate the pious reticence with which this section concludes." [7]

> It is therefore more certain, and less hazardous, to await the fulfilment of the prophecy, than to be making surmises, and casting about for any names that may present themselves, inasmuch as many names can be found possessing the number mentioned; and the same question will, after all, remain unsolved. . . . We will not, however, incur the risk of pronouncing positively as to the name of Antichrist; for if it were necessary that his name should be distinctly revealed in this present time, it would have been announced by him who beheld the apocalyptic vision (Irenaeus *Against Heresies* V. xxx. 3).

Moreover, in a passage where Irenaeus attempts to establish the authority of the apostolic tradition as it had originated in the Roman church and was passed down to their successors, he accomplishes this purpose without reference to the martyrdom of Paul, Peter, or any other of the apostles, and without allusion to the Roman church's having undergone persecution at the hands of the emperor. Irenaeus calls attention to Clement of Rome, who lived in Rome about the time Revelation was written, and in so doing makes no hint of persecution of Christians either there or in Corinth, to whom Clement had written. He also mentions Polycarp's martyrdom in such manner as to suggest that this was the *unusual,* rather than the usual, fate of the Christians in Asia Minor.

Before conclusions are drawn with respect to the value

of Irenaeus for the interpretation of Revelation, however, attention should be called to a passage by Eusebius, the church historian, in which he explicitly claims that Revelation grew out of a political-religious conflict with the Roman authority under Domitian.

> At this time, the story goes, the Apostle and Evangelist John was still alive, and was condemned to live in the island of Patmos for his witness to the divine word. At any rate Irenaeus, writing about the number of the name ascribed to the anti-Christ in the so-called Apocalypse of John, states this about John in so many words in the fifth book against Heresies.[8]

It is somewhat evident that the passage from Eusebius is governed by two factors: (1) the combination of a quotation from Irenaeus with one from Revelation 1:9-10; and (2) Eusebius' desire to portray the glorious side of the early church through calling attention to sufferings faithfully endured. But it has already been shown that Irenaeus does not suggest a Domitian persecution; and the passage from Revelation can be interpreted in a way different from that offered by customary exegesis. By changing the position of only one period, Revelation 1:9-10 may be made to read in an entirely different manner. And this change in punctuation is perfectly legitimate when one recalls that the author of Revelation — as did the other New Testament writers — left his work without any punctuation, and even without any separation between words.

If this change in punctuation is made, the passage then reads, "I John, . . . was on the island called Patmos. On account of the word of God and the testimony of Jesus, I was in the Spirit on the Lord's day." John's words must, then, be taken to indicate that the revelation which he received was given to him while he was *in the Spirit*. This revelation would be a direct rebuttal against his gnostic opponents, who claimed to possess revelations which came to them while they were under the influence of the Spirit.

And this rebuttal is not unlike Paul's attack on his gnostic foes at Corinth (2 Corinthians 12).

We may now summarize the conclusions from our investigation of Irenaeus' writings relevant to Revelation.

(1) Irenaeus is an important source as far as dating Revelation is concerned; there is no real reason to doubt his Domitian date.

(2) It must be recognized that Irenaeus in no wise suggests a connection between Revelation and an assumed Domitian persecution. Nor does Irenaeus suggest that the apostle John or any other Christians were persecuted or suffered martyrdom for their faith during this period. He does state explicitly that the apostle lived until the time of Trajan (Irenaeus *Against Heresies* II. xxii. 5), which could suggest that the Patmos exile, if it must be taken literally, was not too severe an ordeal for the apostle. In fact, it may be that the difficulties under Domitian were not as bothersome as many would like to believe.

> Apparently Domitian (A.D. 81-96) in his later days took this worship more seriously than any of his predecessors save Gaius (Caligula). But though it is commonly said that he conducted a persecution of Christians because of their refusal, there is no evidence of an imperial edict from him enforcing the cult against Christians. The correspondence between Trajan and Pliny in Bithynia in the early second century indicates that Christians were under suspicion and had occasionally at least been executed. Ignatius' well-known difficulty in becoming a martyr indicates, however, that even in his time there was no sweeping attempt.[9]

(3) For Irenaeus, the theological and exegetical significance of Revelation is its absolute lack of connection with a polemical-political situation and its specific connection with an antignostic polemic. It must be acknowledged, however, with respect to this last conclusion, that Irenaeus also uses other biblical writings, especially Daniel, in his antignostic polemic. Yet it does not necessarily follow that

the *original* purpose of Revelation was antignostic, any more than it does that Daniel and the other sources Irenaeus uses were antignostic in their original intent. Still it is valid to maintain that, even though Irenaeus' use of Revelation *does not make certain* an antignostic background for Revelation, it nevertheless *leaves open the possibility* of this approach. Especially is this true when one notes that Irenaeus quotes a tradition concerning the apostle John (whom he considers to have been the author of Revelation), in which is conveyed the apostle's deep feelings against the gnostic Cerinthus.

> . . . John, the disciple of the Lord, going to bathe at Ephesus, and perceiving Cerinthus within, rushed out of the bath-house without bathing, exclaiming, "Let us fly, lest even the bath-house fall down, because Cerinthus, the enemy of the truth, is within" (Irenaeus *Against Heresies* III. iii. 4).

The evidence of Irenaeus, when taken in isolation, is of minimal and negative value for determining the original background of Revelation. It merely affirms that the customary contemporary-historical approach does *not necessarily* uncover the historical setting of Revelation. Yet when the evidence of Irenaeus is considered in light of some difficulties of the present formulation of the contemporary-historical approach, and when a series of gnostic motifs is seen dispersed throughout Revelation, it would seem to indicate that there is some valid basis for understanding these symbols as the partial ingredients of an antignostic conflict.

Other difficulties involved in the customary interpretation of Revelation. It will be of some value to allude to a few of the other difficulties involved in the generally accepted method of interpreting Revelation, although discussion of the exegetical difficulties will be retained until the exposition.

By this method, Revelation 2 — 3 is severed from connection with what follows, a division for which there is no textual or other evidence. Why can the representatives of this approach see so many references to Jewish and gnostic problems in Revelation 2 — 3 and simultaneously fail to recognize any further reference to these same problems in the remaining chapters? An interpretation of this nature can lead only to an understanding of a few figures, but never to the total understanding of Revelation.

This polemical attitude toward the Roman power does not reflect what is known elsewhere about the feeling of the New Testament writers and of 1 Clement, who wrote from Rome about the same time that Revelation is believed to have been written from Asia Minor. Neither the sayings of Jesus (Matthew 22:15-22; Mark 12:13-17; Luke 20:20-26), nor the words of Paul in Romans 13:1-7, nor the teachings of 1 Peter 2:13-14 demonstrate such a hostile attitude toward the state as many believe to be reflected in Revelation. Yet in the section of Revelation which *must* be recognized as speaking to its contemporary situation (2 — 3), there is no political hostility, but only hatred toward the "synagogue of Satan" (2:9), "Satan's throne" (2:13), the "works of the Nicolaitans" (2:6, 15), and the "woman Jezebel" (2:20-23). In what respect do these relate to political hostilities?

A third general difficulty arises in connection with the equating of Babylon with Rome and the Roman power. This will be dealt with further in the exposition, but it is worthwhile here to point out that the description of the beast seated upon seven mountains may as easily have its counterpart in an apocalyptic passage such as 1 Enoch, as in the analogy of Rome, which was built upon seven hills.

> And here I saw seven stars of the heaven bound together in it, like great mountains and, flaming as with fire. . . . Uriel, one of

the holy angels . . . said . . . "These are the stars, which have transgressed the commandment of God and are bound here till ten thousand ages . . ." (1 Enoch 21:3-6).[10]

In view of the fact that the Revelation of John is more than a link in a chain, one may expect from it a purpose and outlook different from that of the earlier, Jewish apocalypses. If it can be shown that the second and third chapters of Revelation relate directly to a gnostic problem, rather than to a persecution under Rome, it is logical to expect further antignostic elements in the remainder of the book. It is to this task that the present undertaking is dedicated.[11]

The approach toward Revelation that will be pursued in the pages following is based upon the assumption that Revelation reflects the *religious* struggles of the author and his readers, rather than the political dangers generally thought to be the setting for the book. And it is further maintained that the religious struggle is against a gnostic group (or groups) who had entered the churches of Asia Minor, claiming to have a "more mature" expression of Christianity. What these gnostics considered to be the ultimate experience of the Christian religion, the author of Revelation believed to be the ultimate deceit of the devil.

REδISCOVERIIG
the
Relevance
of the
seven Letters

THE MOST SIGNIFICANT QUESTION REGARDING THE SEVEN
churches concerns both their basis of selection and their
connection with one another and with other Christian
communities. Generally, one of the three following reasons,
or a combination of them, is put forth as the reason for
their selection. (1) They represent the totality of Christianity in their time; or (2) they are the foremost representatives of the churches in their particular geographical
regions; or (3) they are to be understood as the individual
churches themselves. This last theory needs no elaboration, since it is axiomatic that the author has related the
spiritual condition of each church addressed to its geographical setting and historical background. But this observation does not answer the larger question regarding
the author's reason for selecting *these specific churches* as
the seven; and this is the question which the interpreter of
Revelation must answer.

Representative of Christendom

In itself this approach is pursued in several directions.
Some interpreters take it to mean that the number seven,
symbolic of completeness, indicates that the judgment of
Christ upon the individual churches was meant as the

21

plumbline for all the Christian communities in Asia Minor.[1] Ernst Lohmeyer points out that there is a very real historical reason why these churches in Asia Minor can be understood as the embodiment of the churches of that day, inasmuch as Asia Minor was then the outstanding Christian center and could, therefore, be looked upon as the representative of Christianity.[2] In a more extreme application of this thesis, it is suggested that what is said to these churches is valid for all time, since by the number seven they were made to represent the church throughout history.[3]

There is no basic reason for doubting that John's choice of the number seven was conditioned by his understanding of that number as signifying divine completeness. But this assumption is insufficient to explain the manner in which churches were chosen to be included in the seven. Consequently, among the reasons suggested for the selection of the seven churches, only the second really attempts to answer the basic question *why these particular churches* were chosen as *the seven.*

Foremost Representatives of the Churches in Each Region

The theory which William Ramsay formulated in his definitive work, *The Letters to the Seven Churches of Asia,* generally has been followed as the most acceptable solution of the problem.

Ramsay observed that previously it had been believed that the selection of the seven churches was made for the first time with the writing of Revelation. However, he was convinced that Revelation 1:4 and 1:11 made it obvious that these seven were already known as the "seven Asian churches" before John received his vision about them. Ramsay concluded that it must have come about as the churches of the great province of Asia gradually consolidated and organized, so that seven groups came into existence, and at the center of each area was one of the seven churches. This process was completed before John wrote. Ramsay also believed there must already have existed a general agreement with respect to the representative character of the seven churches, or else it is impossible to see how John could have written to these without further explanation, and it would be assumed that his words applied to all.

Earlier in his book, Ramsay had stated that the church owed its growth and unification within the early empire to the fact that it maintained frequent correspondence between the various scattered congregations. Because no postal system was operated by the state for them, the Christians developed means for carrying their own letters. The letter-carriers' routes were marked out in the most convenient circuits, so that the provincial messengers did not visit all the cities, but only those that were central. From these centers a subordinate service carried the letters or news to the other churches in the area.

In this theory two related conclusions are reached: (1) Several messengers were used simultaneously to carry the news intended for the province of Asia. (2) One must have started from the capital (Ephesus), while others went on secondary routes receiving the message from the primary messenger at designated stations along his journey.

> Now, if we combine this conclusion with our previously established results, the hypothesis inevitably suggests itself that the Seven groups of Churches, into which the Province had been divided before the Apocalypse was composed, were seven postal districts, each having as its center or point of origin one of the Seven Cities, which (as was pointed out) lie on a route which forms a sort of inner circle round the Province.[4]

Finally, Ramsay divided the province of Asia into seven districts and affirmed that these cities were the best points on the circuit to serve as the communication centers with the seven areas: Pergamum served the north (Troas, Adramyttium, and perhaps Cyzicus and other coastal cities had churches within their bounds); Thyatira served as the center for an island district at the northeast and east; Sardis was the representative for the wide valley of the Hermus; Philadelphia had the honored position in Upper Lydia; Laodicea mediated for the Lycus Valley and for Central Phrygia, of which it later became the Christian metropolis; Ephesus was the foremost representative on the circuit which incorporated the Cayster and Lower Maeander Valleys and coasts; and Smyrna was the liaison for the Lower Hermus Valley and the North Ionian coasts, perhaps with Mitylene and Chios (if these islands had as yet been reached).[5]

Theological Reasons

Ramsay's thesis is quite enticing and very ingenious. The questions are answered which he felt could be raised because of the omission from Revelation of Troas, Tralles, and Magnesia, the cities of Caria, and those of northern and eastern Phrygia. Yet the basic issue involved is not the possibilities or impossibilities of this as a geographical theory, but whether these considerations should be considered the *primary* criteria for the selection of these particular cities. In view of the fact that no corroborating evidence supports the contention that Asia Minor had been divided into regions for postal circulation, Ramsay's theory loses much of its weight.

On the other hand, one is on much firmer ground when *theological* reasons are sought as the criteria for the selection of the seven churches. This approach receives further justification from the existence of other Christian writings directed toward this same area, which had theological reasons for their geographical references. Moreover, other New Testament writings (*e.g.*, 1, 2, 3 John; 1, 2 Timothy; Jude; 2 Peter) directed to this same general region reflect the same difficulties faced by the churches in Revelation 2-3. These factors combine to suggest that the most satisfactory solution of the problem regarding the choice of the churches must ultimately be related to certain underlying theological difficulties which they faced; and it is tempting to interpret these theological issues in light of an insurgence of persons with gnosticizing tendencies.

Walter Bauer contends that John sought out from among the churches in his vicinity the most noted of those which would still allow him to exert a positive influence.[6] The intimate knowledge that John had concerning the churches suggests that he was not at all unfamiliar with their spiritual life; and therefore he may have possessed special authority in these churches.

It is enlightening to notice that the same areas are not mentioned in 1 Peter, and evidently they were bypassed in the journeys of Ignatius. This omission has generated various assumptions. Moffatt admitted it was just as problematic to understand the reason for Peter's omission of Cilicia, Pamphylia, and Lycia as it was to explain satisfactorily why John chose the seven churches.[7] Hort suggested that the names occur in such an order as one would expect the bearer of the letter to take in visiting the provinces, beginning at Sinope and then making a circuit, returning to Bithynia.[8] But this still does not explain *why* Peter chose to mention these particular locales, while leaving out the names of other areas to which the letter was to be taken. It is more reasonable to assume that these were the *only* intended recipients of the letter, rather than to hypothesize that these were points from which the letter was to be distributed elsewhere.

Windisch conjectures that Peter perhaps intended to include the entire area of Asia Minor. But still it is striking that he omitted Lycia, Pamphylia, and Cilicia. However, Windisch concludes that Peter may have omitted Lycia because there were no significant churches in that region; that probably Pamphylia was intended to be included in Galatia; and that Cilicia was omitted because it belonged to Syria.[9] It is not too convincing to say that Phrygia was to be included in Asia, although this may have been valid for the Roman administration. For this same Roman provincial arrangement had united Pontus with Bithynia; and these are differentiated as much as possible by Peter, since one begins his listing, and the other, separated by three other names, concludes it.

The easiest way to explain the "blank spots" in 1 Peter's geography is to conclude that there is nothing that can be learned about the ecclesiastical Christianity of those areas at the time Peter wrote. In southeast Asia Minor, bordering on Syria, and from the west on as far as Phrygia, no interference with the church life was permitted. Even Clement of Rome, who spoke with authority to the church at Corinth, did not address himself to this region when he wrote later in the same generation. All this is to say that the most satisfactory solution of a complex problem is to conclude that Peter wrote only to those areas which still acknowledged his authority in their ecclesiastical affairs. This explanation will become even more evident as Bauer's thesis is further expanded.[10]

In this regard the letters and travels of Ignatius are as significant as the letter of 1 Peter, if not more so. Ignatius addresses only three of the churches which John mentions: Ephesus, Smyrna, and Philadelphia. Is it by chance that the two churches that are praised the highest, and appear less infested with heretics in Revelation 2 — 3, are those of Smyrna and Philadelphia? Is it merely by accident that the churches of Pergamum, Thyatira, Sardis, and Laodicea — in which are the Balaamites, the Nicolaitans, Jezebel, and those which "know the deep things of Satan" (2:24) — are the churches *not* addressed by Ignatius?

Ignatius could have gone through Laodicea and Sardis on his last journey, as well as through Philadelphia and Smyrna; yet he visited neither of these first-named cities. Revelation records that in Sardis there were only a few who had not "soiled their garments" (3:4). Also in Thyatira, which the traveling Ignatius could have reached as easily as Ephesus, Tralles, and Magnesia, John considers the heretics to be in the majority and the faithful but a small remnant (2:24). In light of these observations, it is not too much to assume that, in Ignatius' day, in the communities of Pergamum, Thyatira, Sardis, and Laodicea there was no bishop to whom he could turn for help in resisting the heretics.

The truth of this judgment may be further corroborated through a brief glance at the early history of the Ephesian church, which both for John and for Ignatius held a position of prominence. Ephesus could not be considered the center of orthodoxy; rather, it was an example of the way in which the life of a church, even one established by an apostle, could shift easily from orthodoxy to heresy.

In the midst of much difficulty, Paul established a church in Ephesus (Acts 19). From Romans 16, a fragment from a letter thought by many to have been written originally to Ephesus, it can be seen that even in the lifetime of Paul false teachers had gained a footing and threatened the life of the church with division. In 1 Corinthians 16:9 is Paul's lament because of the "many adversaries" he faced in

Ephesus; and in Acts 20:30 is his warning to the Ephesian church leaders about those from within their own number who would try to lead away the people by speaking false things. It is quite likely that Paul's words should be taken as an accurate description of the situation in Ephesus at the time Acts was composed. Ignatius also knew of difficulties at Ephesus, for he sent the Ephesians praise because of the way they had stopped-up their ears to the false teachers who had entered their ranks.[11]

From Revelation it appears as if John either did not know of Paul's labors in founding the church at Ephesus, or else he intentionally suppressed the fact. In any case, the statement that they had "forsaken their first love" is a reminder that they had known better times. Only the names of the twelve apostles are placed on the foundation stones of the New Jerusalem (21:14); there is no room for Paul. After a few years the apostle to the Gentiles was disowned by the Ephesian church in favor of John. The message and authority of Paul had proven to be too weak to drive the enemies of the church from the field.

In this connection the Pastorals are important. As a general rule, the Paul of the Pastorals fought along with the church against the inroads of heresy; and the Pastorals agree with Revelation that at the end of the first century, and at the beginning of the second, the apostle had lost the struggle. Onesiphorus received praise because of his special efforts in Ephesus (2 Timothy 1:16-18); yet it is granted in that letter that his efforts had accomplished nothing, for everyone in Asia had deserted Paul (1:15). Even Onesiphorus himself had given up the battle in order to seek out the apostle in Rome (1:17). All that can be learned of the Ephesian church denies that the victory in Ephesus belonged to Paul.

What came about in Asia Minor after the time of Paul

and before John is best explained in terms of a Jewish-Christian migration from Palestine. Jewish Christians, who no longer felt secure in the Holy Land and east of the Jordan, wandered far until they found a new home. Philip, the evangelist, moved from Jerusalem to "a city of Samaria" because of the persecution following the death of Stephen (Acts 8:5). From there he went on to Hierapolis, accompanied by his prophesying daughters.[12] John, the disciple of the Lord, perhaps also exchanged Jerusalem for Ephesus.

This Jewish Christianity, no longer circumscribed by the limitations of the Law, and determined to proclaim its faith effectively in a predominately Gentile world, adopted the terminology of the religious and philosophical systems about it as the means of expressing the truth of its faith. The most readily available and the most flexible was the terminology of gnosticism. It is not to be doubted that much of the Judaism of this period had already subscribed to certain gnostic terminology so as to make its faith more acceptable to the surrounding peoples. Perhaps the same thing that Philo had done in Alexandria was in a sense duplicated by the Jews of Asia Minor in relation to their particular historical context. They began to understand the Old Testament allegorically so as to make it more relevant to the non-Jews, and to emphasize or deemphasize certain elements of their religion so as to make it more intellectually acceptable to those about them. Thus it is possible that the Jewish-gnostic syncretism had begun, at least in some degree, before Christianity entered this region.

When this Jewish-Christian movement entered Asia Minor, certain gnostics (among whom were apparently a number of Jewish descent) were attracted by what appeared to be a more adequate gnostic system and were "converted" (as, for example, Simon Magus was "converted," Acts 8:9-24). What eventually ensued was: (1) a breakdown of the previously existing barrier between Jewish and Gentile Christianity because of the now common grounds of communication; (2) an "orthodox" Christianity which used gnostic terminology only to clothe its message for purposes of communication and polemics; and (3) a "heretical" gnostic Christianity of Jewish tint.

It is this last-named condition that Revelation 2-3 sees in the Asian churches addressed, and that the remainder of Revelation combats by the use of terminology current in gnostic circles. The seer directs himself to *these seven churches* because he considers them the outstanding churches in that area which still may follow his pleas to turn from the influence of the gnostic heresy.

REDISCOVERING
the
GNOSTIC
PROBLEM

THE TASK OF DEFINING GNOSTICISM IS DIFFICULT BECAUSE OF
the "problems of terminology," [1] since no two students of
gnosticism give precisely the same meaning to the term.[2]
Bultmann understands gnosticism as a "synthetic phenom-
enon" which may be described as a "redemptive religion
based on dualism." [3] And he also realizes, along with Jonas,
that all its mythology as well as its theology arises from
a definite perspective toward life and an interpretation of
human experience.[4] Wilson acknowledges that "the characteristic of Gnosticism in all its forms is syncreticism," yet
will also agree that this syncretism is derived from a defined
outlook toward life:

> There is in consequence no one uniform set of ideas that may be
> singled out as Gnostic; rather it is a matter of a type of thought
> which manifests itself in different ways in different groups. Yet
> there are certain characteristic features which reappear in different
> forms and combinations in the different systems, ideas assimilated
> from various sources and not always co-ordinated into a consistent
> scheme.[5]

Any definition of gnosticism, then, must recognize two
factors: (1) Gnosticism is syncretistic by nature.[6] (2) All
the differing gnostic systems possess the same basic outlook
on life which makes them kin to one another. For this
reason the definition offered by Dodd and followed by Wilson is quite accurate with its interpretation of gnosticism

"as a label for a large and somewhat amorphous group of religious systems described by Irenaeus and and Hippolytus in their works against Heresy . . . and similar systems known from other sources." [7]

However, for purposes of our study it is necessary to go beyond this to a more detailed discussion of the basic characteristics which remain intact in all the varying systems.

The Gnostic Understanding of Man

It is fitting to begin a discussion of gnosticism with its interpretation of man and his role in the world, inasmuch as "gnosis is in the final sense anthropology." [8] Man is the center of gnostic thought. Gnostic myths and doctrines describe the origin of man and his purpose for being and point the way he must follow, namely, the way to himself, which in the final analysis is the way to salvation. [9] Leisegang quotes a gnostic fragment in which the essence of gnosticism is given as the "recognition who we are and what we have become; from whence we originate and whither we go; whither we hasten and wherein we are redeemed; what birth is and what rebirth is." [10]

A basic thesis of every known gnostic system is that man does not belong to this world, but rather to a higher, heavenly world. [11] At this point gnosticism differs from both the biblical and the classical Greek views. The Bible looks upon man as originally created in the image of God in a world that was essentially good; the classical Greek view is that man is an intelligent and meaningful being in an orderly universe. But in gnosticism man is no longer at peace with the world; rather, he is imprisoned among the materials of human existence. It is impossible for man to achieve his true realization within the confines of this evil world. [12]

In order to understand the condition of man in the present world, it is necessary to know of his heavenly origin and of his fall. Though the systems differ in their theories regarding the way in which man came into this present condition and how he is to escape, they all agree that his present situation is abnormal because of his fall from a world above. A glance at two systems will indicate their unity of outlook in this despite their diversity of expression.

The *Apocryphon Johannis*, contained in the fifth-century papyrus known as Berolinensis 8502, speaks of the divine origin of mankind and of the evil present in which he exists. A series of emanations takes place until Yaldabaoth, one of the lower emanations and the illegitimate offspring of Heleleth, creates the material world. The invisible God (*i.e.*, the highest God) tricks Yaldabaoth into breathing a divine spark into the creatures he has created so the divine spark can be liberated and returned to the heavenly world. From here on a conflict develops between the true God, who seeks to restore the divine spark to the world above, and Yaldabaoth, who attempts to keep all creatures ignorant of their divine origin.

Simon Magus, the Samaritan magician whom the early church fathers believed to have been the source of all heresy, makes a similar claim for the present status of his female consort Helen. Helen is venerated as the first emanation, the creative Thought. She comes forth from Simon; creates the world; descends to it; and finally becomes imprisoned here by the powers of evil until she falls to prostitution. Finally, Simon descends to redeem her from the material existence and likewise to redeem all others who would follow him and his teaching.

Seen, then, in two divergent mythical forms, are the same basic ideas regarding the heavenly origin of man and his present dilemma.

Because of his fallen condition man must assume that the world is unfriendly and antagonistic to him. There is a "radical difference between man and the world in which he lives." [13] The world has forsaken its divine order and has become demonic. Man and the world are no longer commensurable; man is kin to the divine and unlike the world in which he must live. He is both an immortal soul and a mortal body bound together into one. So radical is the gnostic thought that it pronounces evil every natural impulse and desire by which one is bound to the world, and it affirms that one cannot realize his true self on this earth.[14]

Because not all men respond to the gnostic proclamation, there is a separation among men as well as within the individual man himself. Sometimes the classes of men are interpreted to be three,[15] and sometimes four,[16] but as a rule the divisions are two: the spiritual and the unspiritual. Only the spiritual man is certain of redemption; he is the consecrated gnostic. For the unspiritual there is no hope of salvation.

The Gnostic Understanding of Redemption

Gnosticism is essentially a religion. Even its anthropology is a handmaiden pointing the way to salvation, to God, and to one's true self. Generally this journey of salvation is described in spatial terms: Man on earth goes after death on a heavenward journey through the lower spheres of planets guarded over by divine beings until he attains, by a password, the highest heaven. Although this journey may be given in spatial terms, it is simultaneously considered to be an inner route to one's self.[17]

Since redemption is only for one's spirit or true self and comes after death, it must be conceived as a purely eschatological event:

> Redemption cannot be conceived as a real event in this world at all. . . . Hence redemption must be an absolutely eschatological event, a breach, a dissolution or separation of the real Self from the body and soul.[18]

This is, of course, not an eschatology in some sense as the New Testament speaks of eschatological events;[19] nevertheless it is a real eschatology, apart from which there is no complete redemption.

Through preaching one hears the message of salvation; but, for the gnostic, this message cannot be for all, since only the spiritual can recognize the spirit. He reads the Scriptures with eyes not possessed by others; he hears the message with ears others than those of the natural man. When it is asked what the spiritual person possesses so as to grant him this insight, the answer is *gnosis* ("knowledge").

Gnosis is not simply theoretical knowledge. It is, rather, knowledge that deals with what has already taken place; that is, the gnostic recognizes who he is and what his destiny is to be. It is not like the intent of the mystery cults, to bestow upon the initiate a divine nature by some magical act, but to permit him to recognize his divine origin and the path back of it.[20] The spiritual man is divine by means of his origin; he does not become divine through a mystic experience.

Only this *gnosis* frees the spiritual man from the chains by which the demons have bound him; only through such knowledge can he find the route to his heavenly homeland.

> Gnosis, is not theory, but power, healing, redemption, salvation, freedom, absolute blessedness. Gnosis is the gospel. Gnosis is to the gnostic what faith is for Paul; indeed it is more inasmuch as it goes beyond faith and becomes equated in value with love.[21]

Salvation by *gnosis* is both positive and negative. "Redemption is the negative experience of release from the material as well as the positive experience of taking on the divine nature or likeness, or at the very least coming into the presence of the divine." [22] After the human soul has left the body, it stands directly beneath God and can thus speak to the material body:

> I am a vessel of greater honor than the woman who gave you birth . . . I know myself and acknowledge my origin, and I venerate the unforgettable Wisdom which is in the Father. [23]

The Gnostic Understanding of the World

Intimately related to the gnostic concept of redemption are its ideas regarding the origin and nature of the universe. God, who is otherworldly, invisible, and unrecognizable, stands in opposition to the visible and constantly changing material world. He is the embodiment of perfect goodness; the world is the personification of absolute evil. A basic axiom is that God and the material world stand in an unresolvable contradiction to each other. [24] The gnostic's cosmological speculations must thereby always begin with the question, "How could the good God have brought this evil world into existence?" The answer to this question unfolds the creative process.

Always the process of creation is a movement away from God. Wilson notes that the theories of creation fall into three broad divisions. First, the world could have been created directly by God, or by some lesser power emanating from him. Second, it could have come through the divine word or some other related medium. Third, it could have originated through the fall of some divine being. [25]

These various methods of understanding the origin of the universe can be illustrated by a few brief allusions to some of the gnostic systems. According to the account in Irenaeus, Simon Magus taught that the world had come into existence through beings who had emanated from God. [26]

The *Apocryphon Johannis* and the Valentinian system conceive of the world as due to the fall of a divine being, though the Valentinian system in another instance attributes the creation of the material world to the Wisdom of God, a concept closely related to the Wisdom idea in the Old Testament books of Proverbs and Job, and especially in the apocryphal books of Ecclesiasticus and the Wisdom of Solomon.[27] It is not necessary here to describe in detail any of the many gnostic portrayals of the structure of the universe, which always take the form of some sort of heavenly hierarchy, with the material world at one extreme and the Supreme Being at the other.

The Gnostic Understanding of Freedom

Freedom is a strong eschatological term in gnostic thought. It indicates that the gnostic has attained the goal of his existence if he secures release from the lowly fleshly substance. Freedom is also the "goal"; the free man is the perfect man. It may be that this goal is attained only after death, yet the gnostic is already conscious of himself as a free person. He possesses the *gnosis,* which is spiritual by nature, and which guarantees eternal freedom.

Since the spiritual man sees through the nothingness of the flesh and has already gained release from it, consequently his relation to the world will always be negative. This attitude can express itself in either of two ways: (1) through stringent asceticism, whereby the spotting of his substance through fleshly contact is avoided; or (2) in consequence of the inviolability of his spiritual quality, through the demonstration of his freedom by unrestrained libertinism.[28]

The basis of either libertinism or asceticism is always religious. Hence, neither of these approaches basically involves an ethical problem; they both represent for the gnostic an approach which is defined by his religion. Irenaeus expresses their attitude toward immorality:

> They maintain, therefore, that in every way it is always necessary for them to practice the mystery of conjunction. And that they may persuade the thoughtless to believe this, they are in the habit of using these very words, "Whosoever being *in* this world does not so love a woman as to obtain possession of her, is not of the truth, nor shall attain to the truth" (Irenaeus *Against Heresies* I. vi. 4).

> . . . in order that, as their writings express it, their souls, having made trial of every kind of life, may, at their departure, not be wanting in any particular. . . . no one can escape from the power of those angels who made the world . . . until he has experience of every kind of action which can be practiced in this world . . . (Irenaeus *Against Heresies* I. xxv. 4).

Either asceticism or libertinism pertains to the relationship with the flesh — that void, ungodly, "inhuman" substance that is lifted from the realm of the ethical. Libertinism is but one expression of the battle against the powers of darkness. Van Eysinga refers to the affirmation of the Naasenes, who claimed to know the "deep things," which must be understood by those who commit all sins that they might know the power of Satan and thereby conquer him.[29] This freedom of the spirit from the flesh is the basis of freedom with regard to the flesh:

> For even as gold, when submersed in filth, loses not on that account its beauty, but retains its own native qualities, the filth having no power to injure the gold, so they affirm that they cannot in any measure suffer hurt, or lose their spiritual substance, whatever the material actions in which they may be involved (Irenaeus *Against Heresies* I. vi. 2).

Opposition to Gnosticism in the New Testament

In order to demonstrate that Revelation was not alone in this conflict with the gnostic heresy, let us now turn to a few other New Testament writers who also spoke against a gnosticizing interpretation of the Christian faith.

Evidently the errorists combatted by Jude and 2 Peter are akin to those opposed in Revelation. False teachers, under the guise of Christian prophets (Jude 4a; 2 Peter 2:1 f.), have entered the Christian fellowship. Upon the basis of feigned revelations (termed "empty dreams" by Jude 8) these men participate in pagan feasts and open immorality to declare that illicit physical involvements cannot defile their spiritual nature (Jude 8, 10, 12; 2 Peter 2:10 f.). Not only do they make false distinctions among men (Jude 19), considering themselves "spiritual" and other believers "natural," but they have a distorted view of Christ (Jude 4b; 2 Peter 2:1 f.). In rebuttal, the Christian writers affirm that these men are themselves natural, rather than spiritual, and ought to be excluded from the Christian fellowship (Jude 19, 23). And, in language reminiscent of Revelation, the deceptive prophets are said to have their counterpart in Balaam (Jude 11; 2 Peter 2:15).

Although James is antignostic throughout, the third chapter of his epistle offers the best summary of his polemic. His accusation that many of them (the false prophets) desire to be teachers (3:1) rebukes the gnostics, who claim to be spiritual because of their "wisdom from above." Moreover, the harsh judgment upon the malicious abuse of the tongue in praising God and simultaneously cursing men (3:9f.) has glimmers of the gnostic differentiation between themselves as spiritual (wise) and other men as natural. James contends that the man who is truly wise exhibits this wisdom in purity and humility, rather than in licentiousness and pride (3:13). Through the possession of the true wisdom from above, the content of one's teaching and the quality of one's life are a unity: he who possesses true wisdom exhibits a pure life (3:17).

Of particular interest are the Johannine epistles, inasmuch as these letters apparently were addressed to the same locale as Revelation, and reveal an explicit rebuttal to gnosticism. The terms by which 1 John characterizes God (Light, Love, Life, Truth) were especially prominent among the gnostic religious systems, which described their supreme deity by these titles and referred to the lesser powers as Darkness, Hate, Death, and Lie. First John simply takes over their terminology and applies it to the Christian God as an affront to the pretensions of gnosticism. First John's constant emphasis upon love for one's brother is a reproof of the gnostic tendency to disdain all who are not of the spiritual elite.

Most significant in 1 John is the interpretation of the antichrists as false teachers who deny the basic Christian doctrine that Christ and Jesus are one. It was typical of certain gnostics to maintain that the "spiritual Christ" descended upon the earthly Jesus at baptism, but ascended before the crucifixion, thereby denying a genuine incarnation and destroying the basis of Christian salvation (4: 22-27). First John rightly adjudges that the proper Christian confession must involve the recognition that Jesus Christ is one, and that he experienced both baptism and the cross (5:1-12). Both 2 John and 3 John continue this struggle by warning the readers not to be deceived by the antichrists, who deny the reality of Christ's human body (2 John 7-8).

Many passages in the Pauline epistles (especially 1 and 2 Corinthians, Ephesians, Colossians, and the Pastorals) attest to gnostic conflicts engaged in by the apostle Paul. Rather than undertake a detailed examination of each letter individually, it will fulfill the purpose of this discussion merely to point out certain facets of the gnostic problems that Paul encountered. (1) Although certain of the gnostics whom Paul knew were of the ascetic type (Colossians 2:16; 1 Timothy 4:1 f.; 5:23), most of the difficulties were invoked by those of *libertine* moorings, who felt compelled to participate in open immorality and idolatrous feasts (1 Corinthians 10:14-22; 6:12-20; Philippians 3:17-21; 2 Timothy 3:19; Colossians 3:1 ff.; Titus 1:15), so as to demonstrate that the pure "gold" of their spiritual natures could not be contaminated by any fleshly involvements. (2) It would seem that these gnostics, primarily of *Jewish orientation* (Colossians 1:1-6; 2 Corinthians 11:21 f.; Titus 1:14; 1 Timothy 1:4), placed a value upon circumcision as the seal of their victory over the flesh (Philippians 3:1 f.; Colossians 1:11 ff.). (3) For the evidence of their faith they appealed to *revelations* received by way of visions (Colossians 2:18; 2 Corinthians 12:1), and sometimes Paul himself appealed to visions God had given him as a rebuff to the gnostic boast (2 Corinthians 12:1-10). (4) Finally, as the thesis from which all these other perversions of truth emerged, was the gnostic *dualistic* theology. True, Paul never explicitly refers to this thesis, but it is implied in his constant reminder of the impotency of all "powers" (*e.g.,* principalities, thrones, dominions, authorities) which his readers were tempted to worship, and by the manner in which he calls upon them to look beyond all "powers" to Christ, who is enthroned "Lord of all."

REDISCOVERY
through
REINTERPRETATION

THE FIRST THREE CHAPTERS HAVE INTENDED TO LAY THE
foundation for the interpretation of Revelation to be pursued in this present chapter. In this chapter the imagery
and symbols used in Revelation will be interpreted in light
of the seer's polemic against the gnosticizing movement
which had entered the churches of Asia Minor and was
leading them astray. John uses the terminology of the gnostics to refute their false claims and to establish the truth
of the Christian faith. Throughout this chapter, which of
necessity will be long in proportion to the earlier chapters,
the book of Revelation will be given in the Revised Stan-
dard Version, followed by an interpretation on each passage.

1. *Christ and the Seer (1:1-20)*

1:1 The revelation of Jesus Christ, which God gave him to show
to his servants what must soon take place; and he made it known
by sending his angel to his servant John, ² who bore witness to the
word of God and to the testimony of Jesus Christ, even to all that
he saw. ³ Blessed is he who reads aloud the words of the prophecy,
and blessed are those who hear, and who keep what is written
therein; for the time is near.

4 John to the seven churches that are in Asia:

Grace to you and peace from him who is and who was and who
is to come, and from the seven spirits who are before his throne,
⁵ and from Jesus Christ the faithful witness, the first-born of the
dead, and the ruler of kings on earth.

To him who loves us and has freed us from our sins by his blood

[6] and made us a kingdom, priests to his God and Father, to him be glory and dominion for ever and ever. Amen. [7] Behold, he is coming with the clouds, and every eye will see him, every one who pierced him; and all tribes of the earth will wail on account of him. Even so. Amen.

8 "I am the Alpha and the Omega," says the Lord God, who is and who was and who is to come, the Almighty.

9 I John, your brother, who share with you in Jesus the tribulation and the kingdom and the patient endurance, was on the island called Patmos on account of the word of God and the testimony of Jesus. [10] I was in the Spirit on the Lord's day, and I heard behind me a loud voice like a trumpet [11] saying, "Write what you see in a book and send it to the seven churches, to Ephesus and to Smyrna and to Pergamum and to Thyatira and to Sardis and to Philadelphia and to Laodicea."

12 Then I turned to see the voice that was speaking to me, and on turning I saw seven golden lampstands, [13] and in the midst of the lampstands one like a son of man, clothed with a long robe and with a golden girdle round his breast; [14] his head and his hair were white as white wool, white as snow; his eyes were like a flame of fire, [15] his feet were like burnished bronze, refined as in a furnace, and his voice was like the sound of many waters; [16] in his right hand he held seven stars, from his mouth issued a sharp two-edged sword, and his face was like the sun shining in full strength.

17 When I saw him, I fell at his feet as though dead. But he laid his right hand upon me, saying, "Fear not, I am the first and the last, [18] and the living one; I died, and behold I am alive for evermore, and I have the keys of Death and Hades. [19] Now write what you see, what is and what is to take place hereafter. [20] As for the mystery of the seven stars which you saw in my right hand, and the seven golden lampstands, the seven stars are the angels of the seven churches and the seven lampstands are the seven churches.

The "revelation of Jesus Christ" (1:1) is the theme of the entire composition. By this phrase John indicates his intention to reveal the significance of Jesus Christ in God's creative-redemptive purpose for mankind. In this regard it must not be overlooked that the outline of the book itself unfolds this theme, and that the attributes of the Risen Lord portray him in his relationship to the church (1:5-6), to the unbelieving world (1:7), and, in his overall significance, to the entire created order (1:12-18). John believes that the truth of this revelation will soon be accomplished before the eyes of all men (1:1, 3); but until that moment comes, the Christians of Asia Minor are encouraged to read this "revelation" in their worship assemblies (1:3).

Customarily, 1:9-10 is interpreted to signify that John received his vision while on the isle of Patmos, having been deported there by the emperor Domitian because of his proclamation that Jesus Christ was Lord. But the theory of a Domitian persecution cannot be supported by historical evidence. Moreover, as we have already noted, through a slight change in punctuation this passage is easily understood in light of an antignostic polemic. This change in punctuation is perfectly legitimate, when one recalls that the author of Revelation, as did the other New Testament writers, left his work without any punctuation, and even without any separation between words.

> I, John, your brother
> and fellow-participant in the affliction
> and in the endurance of Jesus Christ,
> was on the island called Patmos.
> Because of the word of God
> and the witness of Jesus,
> I came *in the Spirit* on the Lord's day.[1]

Therefore, these words are intended to emphasize that John received his revelation while *in the Spirit* — a direct rebuttal to his gnostic opponents, who professed to have received revelations while in the Spirit.

In words of poetic grandeur, guided by the vocabulary of the Old Testament, John describes his vision of the Risen Lord and its impression upon him (1:12-16). Recovering from the impact of this vision, John sees its meaning: Jesus Christ is Lord — Lord of history and of the entire created order, Lord over life and death, and Lord of the destiny of all men (1:17-18). The significance of this initial insight is to be unfurled further, and John must record it for a witness to the church and to the world.

2. Christ and His Church (2:1 – 3:22)

2:1 "To the angel of the church in Ephesus write: 'The words of him who holds the seven stars in his right hand, who walks among the seven golden lampstands.

2 " 'I know your works, your toil and your patient endurance, and how you cannot bear evil men but have tested those who call themselves apostles but are not, and found them to be false; [3] I know you are enduring patiently and bearing up for my name's sake, and you have not grown weary. [4] But I have this against you, that you have abandoned the love you had at first. [5] Remember then from what you have fallen, repent and do the works you did at first. If not, I will come to you and remove your lampstand from its place, unless you repent. [6] Yet this you have, you hate the works of the Nicolaitans, which I also hate. [7] He who has an ear, let him hear what the Spirit says to the churches. To him who conquers I will grant to eat of the tree of life, which is in the paradise of God.

Ephesus, situated at the mouth of the Cayster River immediately before it emptied into the Aegean Sea, was the capital of the Roman province of Asia and headquarters of the proconsul. Obviously, the problem faced by the Ephesian church had come from within, rather than from without. False apostles had entered the church and subsequently had been expelled. These men, termed Nicolaitans [2] (perhaps a self-chosen designation to indicate their supposed spiritual strength), are to be identified with the false apostles mentioned in the other letters under the names of Balaamites [3] and followers of Jezebel.[4] It is possible that the defeat of these gnostic errorists had left its mark upon the church. Through their expulsion from the fellowship of the church the gnostic leaders had proved themselves to be "less spiritual" than the Christians they had formerly scorned with pride. Certain weak brothers, hitherto led astray by the gnostic appeal to freedom, had repented and now desired to be restored to the fellowship of the church; but the church frowned upon them in the same way they themselves had formerly reacted toward those who did not go along with them in adopting the gnostic ethic. John refers to this unforgiving attitude on the part of the church as a "fall" from the heart of their faith, and declares that the church will not partake of the reward that belongs to the victor unless they exhibit love toward these "weaker" brothers.

Each section in these seven letters that speaks of the "one who conquers" reflects an antignostic polemic. The gnostic shares in licentiousness and pagan feasts under the pretext that he is strong, and by his indulgence *conquers* the demons and powers that otherwise would subdue him as noted in the previous discussion of gnostic libertinism. The book of Revelation (cf. 2 John 1:14b), reversing this claim, affirms that the one who conquers is not the erring gnostic, but the faithful of the church. In this letter to Ephesus, John promises participation in the "tree of life" (a term used by gnostics) not to the gnostics but to those who overcome the temptation to gnostic libertinism.

8 "And to the angel of the church in Smyrna write: 'The words of the first and the last, who died and came to life.

9 "'I know your tribulation and your poverty (but you are rich) and the slander of those who say that they are Jews and are not, but are a synagogue of Satan. [10] Do not fear what you are about to suffer. Behold, the devil is about to throw some of you into prison, that you may be tested, and for ten days you will have tribulation. Be faithful unto death, and I will give you the crown of life. [11] He who has an ear, let him hear what the Spirit says to the churches. He who conquers shall not be hurt by the second death.'

North of Ephesus on the Aegean coastline lay Smyrna, a city noted for its splendor, wealth, and commercial im-

portance. Christians in that city had to undergo a double
trial, affliction and poverty on the one hand and blasphemy
on the other, and it is likely that the source of both difficulties was the same.[5] Since the gnostics customarily appealed to the rich more than to the poor, it is not improbable that the linking of poverty with the charge of
blasphemy would have originated from conflict with a
(Jewish) gnostic group that rejoiced in its success among
the rich and charged the impoverished Christians with
blasphemy.

Because of their attachment to Judaism, however heretical, these gnosticizing Jews would be recognized by the
Roman authorities as a "legal religion" and conceivably
could make charges against the distinctively Christian
group, causing them trouble within the city; but John
thinks their ability to make trouble is limited, as is inti-
mated by the qualifying phrase "ten days." [6]

The false teachers at Smyrna are described as a "synagogue of Satan." Does John imply that they had termed
themselves the "synagogue of God," but actually were a
"synagogue of Satan," or does this latter phrase represent
the actual claims of these false teachers themselves? [7] The
latter alternative is more probable, for among certain of
the gnostic sects (especially the Ophites, from the Greek
word meaning "serpent") the serpent was venerated as
the Supreme Deity, who had come to reveal to men the
mysteries that would redeem them from the lower Creator
God's attempt to enslave men by his laws.

Several examples will intimate the exalted status of the
serpent among many gnostic groups. Although in the
Ophite sects the role of the serpent varied, some identified
Wisdom herself with the serpent:

> For some of them assert that Sophia [Wisdom] herself became the
> serpent; on which account she was hostile to the creator of Adam,

and implanted knowledge in men, for which reason the serpent was called wiser than all others (Irenaeus *Against Heresies* I. xxx. 15).

Among the Peratae, a kindred group to the Ophites, the serpent, equated with the Word, or Divine Son, made a link between the Supreme Deity and matter:

According to them, the universe is Father, Son, (and) Matter; (but) each of these three has endless capacities in itself. Intermediate, then, between the Matter and the Father sits the Son, the Word, the Serpent . . . (Hippolytus *The Refutations of All Heresies* V. xii).

The Sethians, also of the Ophite strain, identified the perfect Word with the serpent, which entered the defiled womb through deception, so as to redeem the "perfect mind" from the chains that bound it (Hippolytus *Refutation* V. xiv). As a final example, the Cainite sect of the Ophites carried out in the most minute detail the thesis that, inasmuch as the Old Testament God was an evil being, everything that he condemned must be deemed good, and everything that he approved must be considered evil. Thus they honored Cain, Esau, and Korah as their heroes and considered the Sodomites their kin (Irenaeus *Against Heresies* I. xxxi. 1).

In Revelation 2 − 3, it is most profitable to understand the phrase "synagogue of Satan" (and its companion phrases, "throne of Satan," "where Satan dwells," and "deep things of Satan") in light of this serpent theology. When John speaks of the "synagogue of Satan," he has a double connotation in mind. (1) The claim of these gnostics is that they worship the Supreme Deity, whom they identify with the serpent (Satan) of the Old Testament (cf. 12:9). Thus, in the first instance, John simply describes them by their own self-chosen designation. (2) For John, these gnostics would really be a synagogue of Satan, understood in the sense that the Christians of his day interpreted the Genesis account. So the concluding promise may be paraphrased: "He who overcomes the temptation of the Jewish-gnostic error will be able to escape the second death; none other is worthy."

12 "And to the angel of the church in Pergamum write: 'The words of him who has the sharp two-edged sword.

13 "'I know where you dwell, where Satan's throne is; you hold fast my name and you did not deny my faith even in the days of Antipas my witness, my faithful one, who was killed among you, where Satan dwells. [14] But I have a few things against you: you have some there who hold the teaching of Balaam, who taught Balak to put a stumbling block before the sons of Israel, that they might eat food sacrificed to idols and practice immorality. [15] So you also have some who hold the teaching of the Nicolaitans. [16] Repent then. If not, I will come to you soon and war against them with the sword of my mouth. [17] He who has an ear, let him hear what the Spirit says to the churches. To him who conquers I will give some of the hidden manna, and I will give him a white stone, with a new name written on the stone which no one knows except him who receives it.'

In the Caicus River Valley north of Smyrna was situated the inland city of Pergamum. There is no need to assume a persecution of the church by the Roman Government; reference to the death of Antipas is easily understood as the result of mob violence instigated by the false teachers. Indeed, the martyrdom of Antipas must have been an unusual and singular incident, else it would not have received such notice.[8] The burden of this letter most certainly deals with the errors of the gnostics, who by analogy are termed Balaamites and Nicolaitans. In this connection lies the understanding of the death of Antipas and the nature of the retribution promised those persuaded by the gnostic gospel. As Antipas suffered by the sword, so will these false teachers, only this time from the mouth of Christ (cf. 19:16).

Both aspects of the promise to the victor possess but one meaning: care and protection of one's spirit on the journey to the heavenly destiny. The best commentary on this passage comes from a gnostic source entitled Jeu 1:

> When you come to this place, seal yourself with this signet. . . .
> So the watchmen retreat and the curtains retreat until you reach the place of your Father, and he gives you his name and his seal, and you cross over the door into his treasure.[9]

Thus John continues to take up the gnostic promises and reinterprets them in light of his Christian confession.

18 "And to the angel of the church in Thyatira write: 'The words of the Son of God, who has eyes like a flame of fire, and whose feet are like burnished bronze.
19 " 'I know your works, your love and faith and service and patient endurance, and that your latter works exceed the first. [20] But I have this against you, that you tolerate the woman Jezebel, who calls herself a prophetess and is teaching and beguiling my servants to practice immorality and to eat food sacrificed to idols. [21] I gave her time to repent, but she refuses to repent of her immorality. [22] Behold, I will throw her on a sickbed, and those who commit adultery with her I will throw into great tribulation, unless they repent of her doings; [23] and I will strike her children dead. And all the churches shall know that I am he who searches mind and heart, and I will give to each of you as your works deserve. [24] But to the rest of you in Thyatira, who do not hold this teaching, who have not learned what some call the deep things of Satan, to you I say, I do not lay upon you any other burden; [25] only hold fast what you have, until I come. [26] He who conquers and who keeps my works until the end, I will give him power over the nations, [27] and he shall rule them with a rod of iron, as when earthen pots are broken in pieces, even as I myself have received power from my Father; [28] and I will give him the morning star. [29] He who has an ear, let him hear what the Spirit says to the churches.'

Due east of Pergamum, on the road leading to Sardis, was the city of Thyatira, mainly noted for its commerce and trade. The church there was threatened by the influence of

Jezebel, whose teachings were the same as the Nicolaitans', though the reversed order ("to commit adultery" precedes "to eat food offered to idols") signifies her particular emphasis. This name, used symbolically, is chosen because of the similarity between this Jezebel and the Jezebel of Old Testament infamy. As an adherent of this libertine gnostic movement, she perhaps uttered her oracles in a state of ecstasy and propagated her doctrines with shameful orgies, all the while justifying her conduct by the affirmation that these experiences were necessary to know the "deep things of Satan." Analogies between the character and fate of Jezebel and of the woman "Babylon" of Revelation 17 — 18 suggest that the personification of Babylon as a woman could be a macroscopic view of the woman Jezebel!

Jezebel seems to have been active within the Christian community for a long while, and the seer feels compelled to level a fierce threat against her and her followers:

> I am casting her
>   into bed
> and those committing adultery with her
>   into great affliction;
> and I will kill her children
>   with death (2:22).

3:1 "And to the angel of the church in Sardis write: 'The words of him who has the seven spirits of God and the seven stars.

" 'I know your works; you have the name of being alive, and you are dead. [2] Awake, and strengthen what remains and is on the point of death, for I have not found your works perfect in the sight of my God. [3] Remember then what you received and heard; keep that, and repent. If you will not awake, I will come like a thief, and you will not know at what hour I will come upon you. [4] Yet you have still a few names in Sardis, people who have not soiled their garments; and they shall walk with me in white, for they are worthy. [5] He who conquers shall be clad thus in white garments, and I will not blot his name out of the book of life; I will confess his name before my Father and before his angels. [6] He who has an ear, let him hear what the Spirit says to the churches.'

Sardis, like Thyatira to the north, was noted for its manufactured goods. Within the church were a few who had not "soiled their garments" with the antinomian gnostic heresy; these alone would have their names confessed before the Father and share in the rewards of victory. John employed the "book of life" concept, ancient in origin and very likely a part of the gnostic paraphernalia of his day, to combat the insidious claims of the gnostics that they alone have received the teaching from the Father and are qualified to be inscribed in the book of life. In this connection should be interpreted Christ's readiness to "confess the names" of the faithful before the Father, since this represents a frequent theme in gnostic literature. Confession of one's name before the Father is dependent upon a view of Christ which the gnostics do not share.

7 "And to the angel of the church in Philadelphia write: 'The words of the holy one, the true one, who has the key of David, who opens and no one shall shut, who shuts and no one opens. 8 "'I know your works. Behold, I have set before you an open door, which no one is able to shut; I know that you have but little power, and yet you have kept my word and have not denied my name. 9 Behold, I will make those of the synagogue of Satan who say that they are Jews and are not, but lie — behold, I will make them come and bow down before your feet, and learn that I have loved you. 10 Because you have kept my word of patient endurance, I will keep you from the hour of trial which is coming on the whole world, to try those who dwell upon the earth. 11 I am coming soon; hold fast what you have, so that no one may seize your crown. 12 He who conquers, I will make him a pillar in the temple of my God; never shall he go out of it, and I will write on him the name of my God, and the name of the city of my God, the new Jerusalem which comes down from my God out of heaven, and my own new name. 13 He who has an ear, let him hear what the Spirit says to the churches.'

East of Sardis stood the majestic Greek city of Philadelphia, which was in truth a gateway to the east. Philadelphia had within its gates a large number of Jews, as can be perceived both from Revelation and from Ignatius, a Christian leader who addressed a letter to Philadelphia two decades later. From all accounts, there existed a tremendous conflict between the Christian group and the Jews, although no outside authorities appear to have been ushered into the fracas. The problem that Ignatius encountered was a Jewish-gnostic mixture; and it is appropriate to look for the same situation reflected in this letter, especially when antignostic motifs are so numerous in the letters to the other churches.

That the promises within this letter relate specifically to Jewish hopes (3:7b, 9b, 12) is to be expected. Yet the description of the believer as a "pillar" was a frequent term in antiquity outside Judaism, including its occurrence in gnostic literature. It is to be assumed that the Jews, carried away by a false message, would retain certain of their Jewish hopes, though in a modified form. This contention receives justification from the recognition that the Old Testament Scriptures in a perverted form were used by many gnostics. Participation in, and inscription with, the name of God would have been a particularly suitable promise to the faithful, especially in the face of a conflict in which the gnostics claimed to be the only ones who had access to the name of the true God. The *Gospel of Truth* concludes:

> And His children are perfect and worthy of His Name, for they are children such as He, the Father, loves.[10]

14 "And to the angel of the church in Laodicea write: 'The words of the Amen, the faithful and true witness, the beginning of God's creation.

15 " 'I know your works: you are neither cold nor hot. Would that you were cold or hot! [16] So, because you are lukewarm, and neither cold nor hot, I will spew you out of my mouth. [17] For you say, I am rich, I have prospered, and I need nothing; not knowing

that you are wretched, pitiable, poor, blind, and naked. [18] Therefore I counsel you to buy from me gold refined by fire, that you may be rich, and white garments to clothe you and to keep the shame of your nakedness from being seen, and salve to anoint your eyes, that you may see. [19] Those whom I love, I reprove and chasten; so be zealous and repent. [20] Behold, I stand at the door and knock; if any one hears my voice and opens the door, I will come in to him and eat with him, and he with me. [21] He who conquers, I will grant him to sit with me on my throne, as I myself conquered and sat down with my Father on his throne. [22] He who has an ear, let him hear what the Spirit says to the churches.' "

Laodicea, last of the cities addressed, a banking center, was known for its pride and self-sufficiency. Christ's promise that some will share in the meal with him, when taken in conjunction with the reference to those who have defiled themselves, may well indicate a threat against those who were yet participating in the pagan cultic meals. Only those who refrained from the gnostic libertinism would be suitable for the victory meal with Christ at the end of time. Other antignostic echoes, evident in the concluding promise, need no further amplification when interpreted against the background of the gnostic "Redeemer Myth," which will be discussed in relation to Revelation 14.

Summary of the Problem Faced by the Churches. A composite may now be drawn of these errorists, who were the same in all the churches addressed. They shared in a Jewish-gnostic heritage; joined freely in immorality and pagan rites to demonstrate their superiority over the flesh; professed allegiance to Satan (whom they classify above the Creator God); and had their own prophets (figuratively described as Jezebel, Balaam, Nicolaitans). These characteristics will be further illuminated throughout the course of the exposition, demonstrating that the main body of the book of Revelation deals with the same heresy which is countered by the letters to the seven churches.

3. *Christ and the Course of World History (4:1 — 14:20)*

A. WORSHIP AND PRAISE TO THE GOD OF CREATION AND REDEMPTION (4:1 — 5:14)

4:1 After this I looked, and lo, in heaven an open door! And the first voice, which I had heard speaking to me like a trumpet, said, "Come up hither, and I will show you what must take place after this." [2] At once I was in the Spirit, and lo, a throne stood in heaven, with one seated on the throne! [3] And he who sat there appeared like jasper and carnelian, and round the throne was a rainbow that looked like an emerald. [4] Round the throne were twenty-four thrones, and seated on the thrones were twenty-four elders, clad in white garments, with golden crowns upon their heads. [5] From the throne issue flashes of lightning, and voices and peals of thunder, and before the throne burn seven torches of fire, which are the seven spirits of God; [6]and before the throne there is as it were a sea of glass, like crystal.

And round the throne, on each side of the throne, are four living creatures, full of eyes in front and behind: [7] the first living creature like a lion, the second living creature like an ox, the third living creature with the face of a man, and the fourth living creature like a flying eagle. [8] And the four living creatures, each of them with six wings, are full of eyes all round and within, and day and night they never cease to sing,

"Holy, holy, holy, is the Lord God Almighty,

who was and is and is to come!"

[9] And whenever the living creatures give glory and honor and thanks to him who is seated on the throne, who lives for ever and ever, [10] the twenty-four elders fall down before him who is seated on the throne and worship him who lives for ever and ever; they cast their crowns before the throne, singing,

[11] "Worthy art thou, our Lord and God,

to receive glory and honor and power,

for thou didst create all things,

and by thy will they existed and were created."

A door is opened in heaven (4:1), indicating thereby that a divine revelation is about to take place; and John further verifies the divine origin of this revelation by his affirmation that the vision is mediated through the presence of God's Spirit (4:2; cf. below). Central to the scene is God himself, whose appearance John describes only by

analogy, so as to avoid the possibility of making God into
the likeness of any part of the created order. Immediately
surrounding the throne of God are four "living creatures,"
described in words drawn from the inaugural vision of
Ezekiel (Ezekiel 1:5 ff.), representative of the entirety of
God's created order, over which God sits enthroned in
ineffable majesty. With words patterned after the cherubim
of Isaiah's vision (Isaiah 6:1-6), the heavenly creatures offer
unceasing praise to God. Immediately before the throne
are the "seven spirits of God," perhaps symbolic of the absolute holiness of the One upon the throne. An outer circle
is composed of "twenty-four elders," representing a heavenly community of worshipers, whose main function is to
bow in praise before God (4:10-11; 5:8, 11, 14; 7:11; 11:16;
19:4), although certain of them also serve to interpret
various aspects of John's vision (5:5; 7:13).

This scene of the sacred drama reaches its climax in a
hymn of praise to God for his works of creation and redemption (4:11). For the seer, the purpose of his chapter
is to make explicit what is implicit in his every character-
ization of God; that is, the *oneness of Creator and Redeemer.* For orthodox Jews or Christians this was a well
known axiom, but for persons who differentiated between
Creator and Redeemer, as in gnosticism, this would be a
stringent rebuttal. Several aspects of this chapter require
closer examination.

The statement of 4:2, in which the seer states that he
was "in the Spirit," has generated much alarm because of
the apparent contradiction to what he said at the outset
of his writing.[11] Even the introductory words of 4:1 reveal
that the seer considers himself still in the state of ecstasy.[12]
Evidently the prophet has a definite purpose in stating *at
this point* his conviction that it was his possession by the
Spirit that gave him this insight. An affirmation of this

nature would be most appropriate in a polemic against a group who claimed a certain (in this case, cosmological) knowledge because of their possession by the Spirit. With their own weapons John chooses to defeat them. They claim that their *gnosis* concerning God and the universe comes from a special spiritual consciousness, which reaches its height in the ecstatic vision; John claims this authority for himself, and the content of this *gnosis*, as witnessed in this enthronement scene, refutes the gnostic dualism.

In the construction of Revelation, Chapter 4 serves a double purpose. (1) It introduces once and for all the entire apocalyptic section. (2) It forms, along with Chapter 5, to which it is closely related, the prelude to the visions of the seals.[13] These considerations suggest the central place this chapter has in the total writing. By placing the chapter at this location John defines a theology that determines the remainder of the book: *The entire redemptive drama that follows originates from the one God through whose will all things were created.* The Creator in this instance is not one in a series of "powers," one that has fallen from the God of Light, but he himself is the God who sits enthroned in indescribable majesty. All the other powers and creatures in the universe are *below* him and bow in worship before him. In all this John sets his sights upon a dualistic theology which proposes to remove the Creator from the throne and make him one of the lesser powers beneath the world of Light.

This designation of God as the Almighty One is unique to the book of Revelation, where it occurs eight times, except for 2 Corinthians 6:18, where it appears to be a quotation from the Septuagint.[14] The author may have had a particular purpose in mind for using so frequently this special name for God; for, in addition to its presence in this important chapter, it stands both at the beginning

(1:8) and at the end of the book (21:22). Once again John has chosen a title for God that identifies Creator and Redeemer as one, and at the same time combats a theology that grants this ascription to the latter, but not to the former, such as was done among the Ophites and Naasenes.

5:1 And I saw in the right hand of him who was seated on the throne a scroll written within and on the back, sealed with seven seals; ² and I saw a strong angel proclaiming with a loud voice, "Who is worthy to open the scroll and break its seals?" ³ And no one in heaven or on earth or under the earth was able to open the scroll or to look into it, ⁴ and I wept much that no one was found worthy to open the scroll or to look into it. ⁵ Then one of the elders said to me, "Weep not; lo, the Lion of the tribe of Judah, the Root of David, has conquered, so that he can open the scroll and its seven seals."

6 And between the throne and the four living creatures and among the elders, I saw a Lamb standing, as though it had been slain, with seven horns and with seven eyes, which are the seven spirits of God sent out into all the earth; ⁷ and he went and took the scroll from the right hand of him who was seated on the throne. ⁸ And when he had taken the scroll, the four living creatures and the twenty-four elders fell down before the Lamb, each holding a harp, and with golden bowls full of incense, which are the prayers of the saints; ⁹ and they sang a new song, saying,

"Worthy art thou to take the scroll and to open its seals,
for thou wast slain and by thy blood didst ransom men for God
from every tribe and tongue and people and nation,
¹⁰ and hast made them a kingdom and priests to our God,
and they shall reign on earth."

¹¹ Then I looked, and I heard around the throne and the living creatures and the elders the voice of many angels, numbering myriads of myriads and thousands of thousands, ¹² saying with a loud voice, "Worthy is the Lamb who was slain, to receive power and wealth and wisdom and might and honor and glory and blessing!" ¹³ And I heard every creature in heaven and on earth and under the earth and in the sea, and all therein, saying, "To him who sits upon the throne and to the Lamb be blessing and honor and glory and might for ever and ever!" ¹⁴ And the four living creatures said, "Amen!" and the elders fell down and worshiped.

While Chapter 4 is designed to affirm the exalted status

of the Father, Chapter 5 demonstrates the inseparable unity between Father and Son by having the heavenly worshipers render equal homage to them both. Much disagreement exists relevant to the form and content of the sealed scroll,[15] yet it seems quite probable that the scroll is intended to contain the revelation of God's plan for world history and for world redemption to which Christ alone holds the key. Through the recognition and confession of Christ's lordship the church gains a proper perspective of God's activity in human history; and this revelation is now unfolded through the opening of the seals. Also in this passage of poetic grandeur the seer continues his polemic against the gnostic heresy by reminding his readers of an affirmation contradictory to the gnostic viewpoint, albeit integral to the heart of the Christian confession: Christ, who truly died (as a butchered Lamb), is one with the God of creation and redemption:

> "To him who sits upon the throne and to the Lamb be blessing and honor and glory and might for ever and ever!" (5:13)

B. JUDGMENT AND GRACE IN WORLD HISTORY (6:1 — 14:20)

6:1 Now I saw when the Lamb opened one of the seven seals, and I heard one of the four living creatures say, as with a voice of thunder, "Come!" [2] And I saw, and behold, a white horse, and its rider had a bow; and a crown was given to him, and he went out conquering and to conquer.

3 When he opened the second seal, I heard the second living creature say, "Come!" [4] And out came another horse, bright red; its rider was permitted to take peace from the earth, so that men should slay one another; and he was given a great sword.

[5] When he opened the third seal, I heard the third living creature say, "Come!" And I saw, and behold, a black horse, and its rider had a balance in his hand; [6] and I heard what seemed to be a voice in the midst of the four living creatures saying, "A quart of wheat for a denarius, and three quarts of barley for a denarius; but do not harm oil and wine!"

7 When he opened the fourth seal, I heard the voice of the fourth living creature say, "Come!" 8 And I saw, and behold, a pale horse, and its rider's name was Death, and Hades followed him; and they were given power over a fourth of the earth, to kill with sword and with famine and with pestilence and by wild beasts of the earth.

9 When he opened the fifth seal, I saw under the altar the souls of those who had been slain for the word of God and for the witness they had borne; 10 they cried out with a loud voice, "O Sovereign Lord, holy and true, how long before thou wilt judge and avenge our blood on those who dwell upon the earth?" 11 Then they were each given a white robe and told to rest a little longer, until the number of their fellow servants and their brethren should be complete, who were to be killed as they themselves had been.

12 When he opened the sixth seal, I looked, and behold, there was a great earthquake; and the sun became black as sackcloth, the full moon became like blood, 13 and the stars of the sky fell to the earth as the fig tree sheds its winter fruit when shaken by a gale; 14 the sky vanished like a scroll that is rolled up, and every mountain and island was removed from its place. 15 Then the kings of the earth and the great men and the generals and the rich and the strong, and every one, slave and free, hid in the caves and among the rocks of the mountains, 16 calling to the mountains and rocks, "Fall on us and hide us from the face of him who is seated on the throne, and from the wrath of the Lamb; 17 for the great day of their wrath has come, and who can stand before it?"

One of the gnostic presuppositions is that the initiated is able to fathom all mysteries, those relating to the nature of the universe and the goal of history as well as those pertaining to man's salvation. Now, the seer sets out to refute this presumptuous claim by declaring that the knowledge of cosmic and redemptive mysteries belongs only to the church, since it is to the church alone that Christ has revealed these secrets. Because the gnostic's Christology is faulty, all his conclusions founded upon this presupposition are invalid; thus he cannot perceive and evaluate properly God's action in history. Beginning in this chapter, John unfolds the mysteries Christ has made known to the true people of God, and this through apocalyptic symbolism, a technique familiar to his readers and most adequate for his purpose.

Perhaps the seer has chosen the technique of apocalyptic for several reasons. (1) The apocalyptic framework is for him the most adequate way to express the superiority of Christianity over gnosticism. By means of this apocalyptic outline the Christian faith is demonstrated to be, not a void and "timeless myth," but a truly historical religion, with a doctrine of the end of time based upon the historical Christ-event. (2) The gnostics themselves used myths to express their philosophy of life; so the Christian apocalyptist chooses to combat them with their own weapons, as he had done earlier in the "letters to the churches," by taking up their terminology and filling it with Christian content. (3) Finally, he perhaps feels as if the only way to delineate fully the demonic proportions of the gnostic foe, whom he considers to be the ultimate and final resurgence of the antichrist, is through the medium of mythological language, by which his readers can behold the completely demonic origin of this perversion of the truth.

For these reasons it is not to be expected that John would make a *direct* reference to his gnostic opponents in every verse of his writing. By using the apocalyptic form he is able to appeal to their interests in cosmological and soteriological mysteries and to draw their attention to the basic truth he wishes to present: *the one God of the Christian faith is Creator and Redeemer and he makes himself known both by judgment and by grace.* That he makes so many Old Testament references is not only due to his own thorough knowledge of these traditions, but also due to his desire to identify the God of the Old Testament with the God of his Christian faith. However, in several places John makes his polemic more direct and specific, as can be seen in the exposition of the following chapters.

Before entering into an interpretation of any one of the apocalyptic visions, a few preliminary observations regarding the visions as a whole will be valuable.[16] In several aspects the seal-visions (6:1 — 8:1) and the trumpet-visions (8:2 — 11:15) are analogous. Each series is determined by the sacred number seven, as are the later bowl-visions (15:1 — 16:22). Furthermore, the seventh member of each series serves as a literary technique, forming a transition to the following section; the seventh seal introduces the trumpet-visions, while the seventh trumpet prepares for the vision of the ark in the heavenly sanctuary (11:19). Again, there is an interlude between the sixth and seventh vision in each series (7:1-18; 11:1-13). Nevertheless, a significant difference exists in that the seal-visions receive their outline from what apparently was a sevenfold apocalyptic expectation relating to the last days; whereas much of the content of the trumpet-visions (and the bowl-visions) receives its cue from the Exodus account of the plagues. Further reference will be made to this latter observation in the interpretation to follow; but, for the present, attention is directed to the significance each sevenfold series of visions (seals, trumpets, and bowls) has in the total framework of Revelation.

Though each series of visions makes its own unique emphasis, the overall meaning is in some measure the same — the revelation of God's action in the affairs of mankind. For example, the seals contain a symbolic summation of all history, past and present, seen in light of God's judicial and redemptive activity. Throughout the course of human history men of faith have endured suffering (6:9-11), but God knows those who are his (7:1-8) and constantly brings his judgment upon the unbelieving world, which is not able to perceive in its failures the judgment of God (6:1-8, 12-17). The trumpet-visions (8:2 — 11:15) underline God's final action in history, which the seer believes to be imminent, climaxed by the final resurgence of the antichrist (11:15 — 13:18) and the appearance of the Son of Man (14:1-20).

Finally, from the obvious analogy between them, it is safe to conclude that the bowl-visions are intended to be an intensified reworking of the trumpet-visions; that is to say, the seer approaches from another angle the motifs of 8:2 — 11:15. This time, however, the events are final and consummative, whereas the earlier plagues were penultimate and partial. Thereto the same elements follow as in the former series: the final defeat of the demonic forces that lie behind the evil of the world (Babylon, 17:1 — 19:10) climaxed by the appearance of the Word of God and the consummation of all history (19:11 — 22: 19).

Apocalyptic authors habitually adopted, with modified interpretations, the concepts and thought-patterns of their predecessors; and it appears quite likely that the scheme of events in this section (6:1 — 8:1) reflects a traditional formulation that John took over from current Jewish and Christian thought on the subject, inasmuch as both here and in Mark 13 is essentially the same outline of events. However, John wrote his apocalyptic drama so that the symbolic events are made to refer to the course of history in general, rather than being limited to the last times, as in Mark and in Jewish apocalypses. For John, these symbols present a theology of history which affirms that all human history, when viewed properly, verifies the divine presence as effecting both grace and judgment in its midst.

The famous four horsemen of Revelation point to the evil effected by humankind throughout the entire course of history. War (6:1-2) and Universal Strife (6:3-4), indicative of man's rebellion against his Creator, are invariably accompanied by their fearful cohorts, Famine (6:5-6) and Pestilence (6:7-8). Thus these four seals depict the fearsome existence of man in a world conditioned by sin and its retribution; though sinful man recognizes neither for what it is. Amidst all the sin of the world the faithful of God inevitably suffer the hatred of the unbelieving world and cry out to God for relief (6:9-11), which will be granted them in the proper hour. A sixth seal, when opened, indicates that the entire created order rebels at the sin and corruption of man and awaits the redemption of God (6:12-17).

7:1 After this I saw four angels standing at the four corners of the earth, holding back the four winds of the earth, that no wind might blow on earth or sea or against any tree. ² Then I saw another angel ascend from the rising of the sun, with the seal of the living God, and he called with a loud voice to the four angels who had been given power to harm earth and sea, ³ saying, "Do not harm the earth or the sea or the trees, till we have sealed the servants of our God upon their foreheads." ⁴ And I heard the number of the sealed, a hundred and forty-four thousand sealed, out of every tribe of the sons of Israel, ⁵ twelve thousand sealed out of the tribe of Judah, twelve thousand of the tribe of Reuben, twelve thousand of the tribe of Gad, ⁶ twelve thousand of the tribe of Asher, twelve thousand of the tribe of Naphtali, twelve thousand of the tribe of Manasseh, ⁷ twelve thousand of the tribe of Simeon, twelve thousand of the tribe of Levi, twelve thousand of the tribe of Issachar, ⁸ twelve thousand of the tribe of Zebulun, twelve thousand of the tribe of Joseph, twelve thousand sealed out of the tribe of Benjamin.

9 After this I looked, and behold, a great multitude which no man could number, from every nation, from all tribes and peoples and tongues, standing before the throne and before the Lamb, clothed in white robes, with palm branches in their hands, ¹⁰ and crying out with a loud voice, "Salvation belongs to our God who sits upon the throne, and to the Lamb!" ¹¹ And all the angels stood round the throne and round the elders and the four living creatures, and they fell on their faces before the throne and worshiped God, ¹² saying, "Amen! Blessing and glory and wisdom and thanksgiving and honor and power and might be to our God for ever and ever! Amen."

13 Then one of the elders addressed me, saying, "Who are these, clothed in white robes, and whence have they come?" [14] I said to him, "Sir, you know." And he said to me, "These are they who have come out of the great tribulation; they have washed their robes and made them white in the blood of the Lamb.
[15] Therefore are they before the throne of God,
    and serve him day and night within his temple;
    and he who sits upon the throne will shelter them with his
    presence.
[16] They shall hunger no more, neither thirst any more;
    the sun shall not strike them, nor any scorching heat.
[17] For the Lamb in the midst of the throne will be their shepherd,
    and he will guide them to springs of living water;
    and God will wipe away every tear from their eyes."

Revelation 7:1-8 and 11:1-6 fulfill essentially the same function in the overall framework of Revelation. Each in its own manner verifies God's foreknowledge and his protective care for his people. Chapter 7 accomplishes this through the application of "seals" upon the foreheads of the believers (v. 3), thereby separating them from the unbelieving world; while Chapter 11 attests God's protective care through "measuring" the inner court of the Temple — marking it off from profanation by sinful men (v. 1).

It is not at all necessary to seek a reference to martyrdom in the description of the redeemed in this chapter, as those "who have passed through the great affliction and have cleaned their garments by the blood of the Lamb" (v. 14). These same people are earlier identified as those who have come from every race of men (v. 9); and it is much more likely that John wishes his readers to understand these worshipers as the entire redeemed community, rather than as a specialized group of martyrs.[17] Throughout Revelation no special emphasis is placed upon the value of martyrdom, though faithfulness is always demanded, even if it leads to death. Always the Christian writer sees the blessings which later Judaism ascribed to martyrs as belonging to all the people of God. Thereby it is not necessary to seek for a persecution background in this passage or in other passages in the Revelation which mention the rewards of faithful endurance.

8:1 When the Lamb opened the seventh seal, there was silence in heaven for about half an hour. [2] Then I saw the seven angels who stand before God, and seven trumpets were given to them. [3] And another angel came and stood at the altar with a golden censer; and he was given much incense to mingle with the prayers of all the saints upon the golden altar before the throne; [4] and the smoke of the incense rose with the prayers of the saints from the hand of the angel before God. [5] Then the angel took the censer and filled it with fire from the altar and threw it on the earth; and there were peals of thunder, loud noises, flashes of lightning, and an earthquake.

6 Now the seven angels who had the seven trumpets made ready to blow them.

7 The first angel blew his trumpet, and there followed hail and fire, mixed with blood, which fell on the earth; and a third of the earth was burnt up, and a third of the trees were burnt up, and all green grass was burnt up.

8 The second angel blew his trumpet, and something like a great mountain, burning with fire, was thrown into the sea; [9] and a third of the sea became blood, a third of the living creatures in the sea died, and a third of the ships were destroyed.

10 The third angel blew his trumpet, and a great star fell from heaven, blazing like a torch, and it fell on a third of the rivers and on the fountains of water. [11] The name of the star is Wormwood. A third of the waters became wormwood, and many men died of the water, because it was made bitter.

12 The fourth angel blew his trumpet, and a third of the sun was struck, and a third of the moon, and a third of the stars, so that a third of their light was darkened; a third of the day was kept from shining, and likewise a third of the night.

13 Then I looked, and I heard an eagle crying with a loud voice, as it flew in mid-heaven, "Woe, woe, woe to those who dwell on the earth, at the blasts of the other trumpets which the three angels are about to blow!"

With the opening of the seventh seal an interlude of absolute silence intensifies the solemnity of the forthcoming events. Incense, symbolic of the prayers of the people of God, is offered up before the Divine Presence and receives its response in the plagues present in the trumpet blast of the seven angels (8:6 – 11:15). As stated above, both the trumpet- and the bowl-visions receive their outline from the Exodus account of the plagues that fell on Egypt in the early history of God's redemptive activity. This observation gives an added significance to these occurrences. In the ancient world, from which these themes came, it was believed that the history at the end of time would reflect in some measure the beginning of history; indeed, the end of time would actually be patterned after the beginning of time. For example, the picture of the Garden of Eden was often taken over in Jewish apocalyptic literature as a description of the place of future bliss for the righteous; while the final victory of God over his foes was quite frequently described in Jewish circles as a "New Exodus." So it is not at all difficult to imagine how the Egyptian plagues could be thought to have their counterpart in the forthcoming deliverance of God's people from the oppression of the present world, which, as Egypt in times past, enslaves the people of God.

As in the case of the first four seals, so the first four plagues might readily be looked upon as a single vision in four parts which stand closely conjoined. The first plague (8:7) grows out of the account in Exodus 9:23-26, in which hail is said to have fallen upon the inhabitants of the Nile delta region; while the second trumpet-vision reflects both the first and the second Egyptian plagues (Exodus 7:17 ff.). Making the waters bitter (Revelation 8:10-11) reminds one of the turning of the Nile into blood in the course of the first plague brought on Egypt (Exodus 7:17 ff.). Finally, the failure of a third part of the light produced by the sun, moon, and stars has its counterpart in the darkness which fell over all Egypt in the fearsome days of the preparation for the Exodus (Exodus 10:21).

9:1 And the fifth angel blew his trumpet, and I saw a star fallen from heaven to earth, and he was given the key of the shaft of the bottomless pit; ² he opened the shaft of the bottomless pit, and from the shaft rose smoke like the smoke of a great furnace, and the sun and the air were darkened with the smoke from the shaft. ³ Then from the smoke came locusts on the earth, and they were given power like the power of scorpions of the earth; ⁴ they were told not to harm the grass of the earth or any green growth or any tree, but only those of mankind who have not the seal of God upon their foreheads; ⁵ they were allowed to torture them for five months, but not to kill them, and their torture was like the torture of a scorpion, when it stings a man. ⁶ And in those days men will seek death and will not find it; they will long to die, and death will fly from them.

7 In appearance the locusts were like horses arrayed for battle; on their heads were what looked like crowns of gold; their faces were like human faces, ⁸ their hair like women's hair, and their teeth like lions' teeth; ⁹ they had scales like iron breastplates, and the noise of their wings was like the noise of many chariots with horses rushing into battle. ¹⁰ They have tails like scorpions, and stings, and their power of hurting men for five months lies in their tails. ¹¹ They have as king over them the angel of the bottomless pit; his name in Hebrew is Abaddon, and in Greek he is called Apollyon.

12 The first woe has passed; behold, two woes are still to come.

13 Then the sixth angel blew his trumpet, and I heard a voice from the four horns of the golden altar before God, ¹⁴ saying to the sixth angel who had the trumpet, "Release the four angels who are bound at the great river Euphrates." ¹⁵ So the four angels were released, who had been held ready for the hour, the day, the month, and the year, to kill a third of mankind. ¹⁶ The number of the troops of cavalry was twice ten thousand times ten thousand; I heard their number. ¹⁷ And this was how I saw the horses in my vision: the riders wore breastplates the color of fire and of sapphire and of sulphur, and the heads of the horses were like lions' heads, and fire and smoke and sulphur issued from their mouths. ¹⁸ By these three plagues a third of mankind was killed, by the fire and smoke and sulphur issuing from their mouths. ¹⁹ For the power of the horses is in their mouths and in their tails; their tails are like serpents, with heads, and by means of them they wound.

> 20 The rest of mankind, who were not killed by these plagues, did not repent of the works of their hands nor give up worshiping demons and idols of gold and silver and bronze and stone and wood, which cannot either see or hear or walk; [21] nor did they repent of their murders or their sorceries or their immorality or their thefts.

A fifth trumpet-vision attains much more dramatic proportions and is given in more detail than the visions which preceded (Revelation 9:1-12). Yet it, too, is developed from the Exodus account. Awesome creatures, under the leadership of one named "Destroyer," emerge from the darkness of the abyss and attack men with their tails, which are equipped with the stingers of scorpions. That these beastly creatures have the overall appearance of grasshoppers (locusts) and live "five months" (the lifespan of a locust) signifies that the author intends his readers to perceive in this vision a heightened form of the locust plague that attacked Egypt as of old (Exodus 10:12).

Variant in origin is the sixth trumpet-vision (Revelation 9:13-21), which is derived from apocalyptic expectations wherein the final period in history was to introduce an influx of ravaging horsemen who would subdue the entire earth with their terrors (cf. Ezekiel 38:14 ff., whence this belief took its roots). Thus all these plagues are to come upon mankind, who are given the opportunity to repent (9:20); but, like their Egyptian forerunners, they refused God's grace and must partake of the severity of his wrath. By making this comparison John has identified the God of the Exodus with the God who acts now for his people.

> 10:1 Then I saw another mighty angel coming down from heaven, wrapped in a cloud, with a rainbow over his head, and his face was like the sun, and his legs like pillars of fire. [2] He had a little scroll open in his hand. And he set his right foot on the sea, and his left foot on the land, [3] and called out with a loud voice, like a

lion roaring; when he called out, the seven thunders sounded. ⁴ And when the seven thunders had sounded, I was about to write, but I heard a voice from heaven saying, "Seal up what the seven thunders have said, and do not write it down." ⁵ And the angel whom I saw standing on sea and land lifted up his right hand to heaven ⁶ and swore by him who lives for ever and ever, who created heaven and what is in it, the earth and what is in it, and the sea and what is in it, that there should be no more delay, ⁷ but that in the days of the trumpet call to be sounded by the seventh angel, the mystery of God, as he announced to his servants the prophets, should be fulfilled.

8 Then the voice which I had heard from heaven spoke to me again, saying, "Go, take the scroll which is open in the hand of the angel who is standing on the sea and on the land." ⁹ So I went to the angel and told him to give me the little scroll; and he said to me, "Take it and eat; it will be bitter to your stomach, but sweet as honey in your mouth." ¹⁰ And I took the little scroll from the hand of the angel and ate it; it was sweet as honey in my mouth, but when I had eaten it my stomach was made bitter. ¹¹ And I was told, "You must again prophesy about many people and nations and tongues and kings."

Revelation 10:1 − 11:13 forms an interlude between the last two trumpet-visions. The first of these chapters contains at least three motifs: the appearance of the angel, the voice of the seven thunders, and the eating of the scroll by the seer. The presence of the angel seems to be none other than a literary technique for interpreting the meaning of his actions. Apparently the seven thunders are the voice of God, whose decrees no writing can fully contain; thereby the seer is warned against any attempt to reproduce what he has heard. However, there is a message for him to bear to the people. But this message is such that it leaves a fearsome impression upon the seer; it becomes bitter in his stomach, though its initial reception was joyful to him (10:8-9). Once more the author has indicated his dependence upon earlier Jewish traditions for his materials, since the reference to the eating of the book and its effects is used in Ezekiel (Ezekiel 2:8; 3:1-3).

11:1 Then I was given a measuring rod like a staff, and I was told: "Rise and measure the temple of God and the altar and those who worship there, ² but do not measure the court outside the temple; leave that out, for it is given over to the nations and they will trample over the holy city for forty-two months. ³ And I will grant my two witnesses power to prophesy for one thousand two hundred and sixty days, clothed in sackcloth."

4 These are the two olive trees and the two lampstands which stand before the Lord of the earth. ⁵ And if any one would harm them, fire pours from their mouth and consumes their foes; if any one would harm them, thus he is doomed to be killed. ⁶ They have power to shut the sky, that no rain may fall during the days of their prophesying, and they have power over the waters to turn them into blood, and to smite the earth with every plague, as often as they desire. ⁷ And when they have finished their testimony, the beast that ascends from the bottomless pit will make war upon them and conquer them and kill them, ⁸ and their dead bodies will lie in the street of the great city which is allegorically called Sodom and Egypt, where their Lord was crucified. ⁹ For three days and a half men from the peoples and tribes and tongues and nations gaze at their dead bodies and refuse to let them be placed in a tomb, ¹⁰ and those who dwell on the earth will rejoice over them and make merry and exchange presents, because these two prophets had been a torment to those who dwell on the earth. ¹¹ But after the three and a half days a breath of life from God entered them, and they stood up on their feet, and great fear fell on those who saw them. ¹² Then they heard a loud voice from heaven saying to them, "Come up hither!" And in the sight of their foes they went up to heaven in a cloud. ¹³ And at that hour there was a great earthquake, and a tenth of the city fell; seven thousand people were killed in the earthquake, and the rest were terrified and gave glory to the God of heaven.

14 The second woe has passed; behold, the third woe is soon to come.

15 Then the seventh angel blew his trumpet, and there were loud voices in heaven, saying, "The kingdom of the world has become the kingdom of our Lord and of his Christ, and he shall reign for ever and ever." ¹⁶ And the twenty-four elders who sit on their thrones before God fell on their faces and worshiped God, ¹⁷ saying,

"We give thanks to thee, Lord God Almighty, who art and who wast,

that thou hast taken thy great power and begun to reign.

¹⁸ The nations raged, but thy wrath came, and the time for the dead to be judged,

for rewarding thy servants, the prophets and saints,
and those who fear thy name, both small and great,
and for destroying the destroyers of the earth."
19 Then God's temple in heaven was opened, and the ark of
his covenant was seen within his temple; and there were flashes of
lightning, loud noises, peals of thunder, an earthquake, and heavy
hail.

Chapter 11, continuing the interlude between the visions, is easily divided into two sections, the former describing the measuring of the Temple (11:1-6), and the latter depicting the appearance and murder of the two witnesses (11:7-14). Both sections are united through their veiled allusions to "Jerusalem" (11:2, 8), where it was believed by many Jewish Christians that the final apocalyptic drama was to take place. Moreover, the other elements in each section of the chapter suggest their apocalyptic heritage. Since the desecration of the Temple during the war with the Syrians (*ca.* 175 B.C.), the Temple's desecration was understood as a preview of what would be attempted at the end of time, when the enemies of God would again seek to avenge themselves upon God's chosen people. For three and a half years (42 months, or about 1,260 days) the Temple stood desolate, trodden under foot by the Syrians and profaned by their sacrifices to the god of the Syrians, personified in their blasphemous king, Antiochus Epiphanes; and it was felt that the last days would bring another onslaught of a similar nature. This time, however, God himself would intervene so as to prevent this tragedy from being repeated. Indeed, it was an apocalyptic belief of this nature that encouraged the Jews to protect the Temple at all costs in the war with Rome (A.D. 67-70). They firmly believed God would not allow the same fate to come upon his holy people and his sacred sanctuary again, and so they fought to the death. Revelation 11:1-6 adopts this pattern of thought; but the Temple is now placed in a location in the heavens, and its protection is verified by the act of "marking off" the sanctuary by the use of a measuring rod. In this manner the author of Revelation expresses his confidence that throughout the course of the severe and imminent judgment of God upon the world, the believing community will be supernaturally protected.

Still reflecting his knowledge of Jewish apocalyptic traditions, the seer refers to the two witnesses who make their appearance upon the scene (11:7-14). As the reader will immediately notice, these witnesses are patterned after the biblical pictures of Moses and Elijah, who, it was felt in many apocalyptic circles, would reappear before the end of history and would be rejected a second time as they had been rejected in their first appearance. It is to be recalled that our Lord himself was conversant with this tradition, as is indicated through his comparison of John the Baptist with Elijah, "But I tell you that Elijah has come . . . as it is written of him" (Mark 9:13).

In this manner the author affirms his conviction that immediately prior to the last hour of history God would make one final appeal to the men of the world, but this plea would be refused as his original one had been and the world would rejoice at the "death" of these prophets (11:10). It is quite probable that the seer understood himself and the other "prophets" of the Christian community represented in the guise of these prophets of old; thereby he testifies that the perversion and rejection of the contemporary Christian message is tantamount to Israel's rejection of the prophets of old, whose activities he represents in the work of Moses and Elijah.

By the death of these prophets is initiated the final judgment of God in history, the outcome of which is proleptically heralded in the words of 11:15-19: God will be confessed as Lord of all men, his people will be redeemed, and the world judged for its sin.

12:1 And a great portent appeared in heaven, a woman clothed with the sun, with the moon under her feet, and on her head a crown of twelve stars; ² she was with child and she cried out in her pangs of birth, in anguish for delivery. ³ And another portent appeared in heaven; behold, a great red dragon, with seven heads and ten horns, and seven diadems upon his heads. ⁴ His tail swept down a third of the stars of heaven, and cast them to the earth. And the dragon stood before the woman who was about to bear a child, that he might devour her child when she brought it forth; ⁵ she brought forth a male child, one who is to rule all the nations with a rod of iron, but her child was caught up to God and to his throne, ⁶ and the woman fled into the wilderness, where she has a place prepared by God, in which to be nourished for one thousand two hundred and sixty days.

7 Now war arose in heaven, Michael and his angels fighting against the dragon; and the dragon and his angels fought, ⁸ but they were defeated and there was no longer any place for them in heaven. ⁹ And the great dragon was thrown down, that ancient serpent, who is called the Devil and Satan, the deceiver of the whole world — he was thrown down to the earth, and his angels were thrown down with him. ¹⁰ And I heard a loud voice in heaven, saying, "Now the salvation and the power and the kingdom of our God and the authority of his Christ have come, for the accuser of our brethren has been thrown down, who accuses them day and night before our God. ¹¹ And they have conquered him by the blood of the Lamb and by the word of their testimony, for they loved not their lives even unto death. ¹² Rejoice then, O heaven and you that dwell therein! But woe to you, O earth and sea, for the devil has come down to you in great wrath, because he knows that his time is short!"

13 And when the dragon saw that he had been thrown down to the earth, he pursued the woman who had borne the male child. ¹⁴ But the woman was given the two wings of the great eagle that she might fly from the serpent into the wilderness, to the place where she is to be nourished for a time, and times, and half a time. ¹⁵ The serpent poured water like a river out of his mouth after the woman, to sweep her away with the flood. ¹⁶ But the earth came to the help of the woman, and the earth opened its mouth and swallowed the river which the dragon had poured from his mouth. ¹⁷ Then the dragon was angry with the woman, and went off to make war on the rest of her offspring, on those who keep the com-

mandments of God and bear testimony to Jesus. And he stood on the sand of the sea.

In Ephesians Paul writes that the evil powers faced by the community of faith are of a supraearthly nature; and, beginning in Chapter 12, John reminds his readers of the same truth. The ultimate foes of God's people are the demonic forces lying behind the sin present in the visible world, rather than the world itself. And John undertakes to describe this demonic force by the symbol of a dragon. There can be no doubt that the dragon of this chapter and the serpent are one and the same; John makes the identification so that there will be no doubt:

And the great dragon was thrown down, that ancient serpent, who is called the Devil and Satan, the deceiver of the whole world — he was thrown down to the earth (12:9).

One of the primary motifs of this chapter is the defeat of the serpent, which theme John uses to demonstrate, among other things, the absolute impotency of the gnostic serpent deity (cf. 12:7-8). His defeat comes about by the "blood of the Lamb" and the testimony of those who did not love their lives unto death (12:11). Through this passage the seer implies that the defeat of the serpent theology and its attendant docetic Christology is accomplished through a confession that acknowledges both a genuine incarnation and the death of the true Messiah. In order to participate in the heavenly chorus one must be firm in his admission that salvation belongs to the one Creator-Redeemer God and his Christ, not to the docetic Christ of the gnostic creed (12:10). As the serpent of Genesis deceives the entire world, so now does the gnostic serpent doctrine with its postulation of a false messiah (12:9). Evidently John is referring once again to the Ophites, who appealed to the serpent, affirming that the Creator was a lesser being. This is one reason he has gathered together so many Old Testament passages; he seeks to show that the serpent is in nowise the God of goodness, but of evil, and he arises from the abyss.[18]

Yet another medium through which John combats the serpent theology used by the gnostics is the demonstration that the true, heavenly wisdom and the false, earthly wisdom are diametrically opposed to each other. One cannot be a "child of wisdom" and accept the teachings of this gnostic group. An interpretation of the Heavenly Woman of Chapter 12 is quite difficult and many suggestions have been put forth. Some have felt that the woman symbolizes Mary, of whom Christ was born; or Israel, whence came Christ; or even the Church (ideal Israel), which alone holds the mystery to the person of Christ. But there is another interpretation which suits better the context and the polemical situation: The woman is to be understood as the "Wisdom of God." (There appears to be an intended contrast between the Woman [Heavenly Wisdom] of this chapter and the Woman [Demonic Earthly Wisdom] personified by Babylon in Chapter 17.)

Into this passage John has woven a Jewish mythological account in which the "Wisdom of God," personified as a woman, descends upon the earth at the end of time and finds no dwelling place; hence she must flee from the onslaught of unrighteousness (12:13-17). To this traditional story the seer has prefaced another tradition according to which Wisdom, as a mother, gives birth to the Word of God, the Messiah (12:1-6). For the seer, the Word of God and the Messiah are one and the same (19:13); and thus it is affirmed that the true Messiah has his origin in the Wisdom of God.[19] The Messiah (as the Word of God) imparts a saving *gnosis* to those who recognize him and these alone become the "children of Wisdom." On the other hand, the gnostics, who profess to possess a spiritual perception, are blind to the true Wisdom of God and the true Messiah, and by their antinomianism and false Christology "persecute" those who are truly spiritual, the offspring of the "Wisdom of God" (12:17).

13:1 And I saw a beast rising out of the sea, with ten horns and seven heads, with ten diadems upon its horns and a blasphemous name upon its heads. ² And the beast that I saw was like a leopard, its feet were like a bear's, and its mouth was like a lion's mouth. And to it the dragon gave his power and his throne and great authority. ³ One of its heads seemed to have a mortal wound, but its mortal wound was healed, and the whole earth followed the beast with wonder. ⁴ Men worshiped the dragon, for he had given his authority to the beast, and they worshiped the beast, saying, "Who is like the beast, and who can fight against it?"

5 And the beast was given a mouth uttering haughty and blasphemous words, and it was allowed to exercise authority for forty-two months; ⁶ it opened its mouth to utter blasphemies against God, blaspheming his name and his dwelling, that is, those who dwell in heaven. ⁷ Also it was allowed to make war on the saints and to conquer them. And authority was given it over every tribe and people and tongue and nation, ⁸ and all who dwell on earth will worship it, every one whose name has not been written before the foundation of the world in the book of life of the Lamb that was slain. ⁹ If any one has an ear, let him hear:
¹⁰ If any one is to be taken captive,
    to captivity he goes;
  if any one stays with the sword,
    with the sword must he be slain.
Here is a call for the endurance and faith of the saints.

11 Then I saw another beast which rose out of the earth; it had two horns like a lamb and it spoke like a dragon. ¹² It exercises all the authority of the first beast in its presence, and makes the earth and its inhabitants worship the first beast, whose mortal wound was healed. ¹³ It works great signs, even making fire come down from heaven to earth in the sight of men; ¹⁴ and by the signs which it is allowed to work in the presence of the beast, it deceives those who dwell on earth, bidding them make an image for the beast which was wounded by the sword and yet lived; ¹⁵ and it was allowed to give breath to the image of the beast so that the image of the beast should even speak, and to cause those who would not worship the image of the beast to be slain. ¹⁶ Also it causes all,

both small and great, both rich and poor, both free and slave, to be marked on the right hand or the forehead, [17] so that no one can buy or sell unless he has the mark, that is, the name of the beast or the number of its name. [18] This calls for wisdom: let him who has understanding reckon the number of the beast, for it is a human number, its number is six hundred and sixty-six.

The portrayal of demonic powers as beasts enters Revelation under the influence of a certain phase of Jewish apocalyptic thought which ultimately owes its origin to the Babylonian tradition of Tiamat, the primeval monster slain by Marduk, the patron deity of Babylon. After slaying Tiamat, Marduk fashions the universe from her body. In Jewish literature two such monsters are marked off by names: Leviathan and Behemoth (cf. Job 40:15; 41:1). It was believed in some circles that in the beginning these were the foes whom God conquered but did not utterly destroy. One of these beasts dwells in the sea and the other under the earth; but at the end of time they will reappear and oppose the Anointed (Christ) of God. In this forthcoming battle, however, God will win a final victory and afterwards establish a kingdom in which peace and righteousness will reign supreme.

John, who believes himself to be living in the last era of history — indeed, all time subsequent to Christ's first advent is the final era — thereby uses current apocalyptic terminology to describe the demonic foes whom he sees asserting themselves against God and his Anointed. The first beast is the antichrist (13:1-10), the second beast its false prophet (13:11-18), and the dragon, or serpent, is Satan, from whom the antichrist receives its authority.

But to what foes of the church does John address himself? The overall source for many of the details concerning the beasts is the book of Daniel, the Jewish apocalypse *par excellence.* In that book these figures were applied to the

Syrian power, which, during the interbiblical period, sought to coerce the Jews to deny their faith. However, subsequent to the time of Daniel these symbols were applied variously to any and all of God's foes; and in Revelation the seer adds certain insights that enable one to identify the antichrist as the docetic Christ of gnosticism:

> One of its heads seemed to have a mortal wound, but its mortal wound was healed (13:3).

Certainly, this antichrist beast is intended to stand in sharp contrast with the slaughtered Lamb (5:6 f.). Because the death wound is healed, it is likely that the seer intends that his readers discern an inner difference between the true Christ and the antichrist, although there is a certain external similarity. No death has taken place for the docetic antichrist, and, consequently, no victory is achieved from the viewpoint of the Christian author.

In two passages involving the interpretation of the antichrist are gnostic formulas:

> This calls for wisdom:
> let him who has understanding
> reckon the number of the beast,
> for it is a human number,
> its number is six hundred and sixty-six (13:18; cf. 17:9).

The seer says that this conundrum is written for all who know its interpretation; for all others it remains unintelligible. Customarily, the contemporary-historical approach interprets the number 666 as a reference to Nero, who was supposed to return from the dead and persecute the church.[20] But this calculation is based upon the numerical value of Nero's name as written in Hebrew letters, whereas John always makes reference to the Greek alphabet and nowhere alludes to the Hebrew alphabet. Thus it is quite improbable that he intends a veiled allusion to the Hebrew alphabet in this passage.[21]

Among the Pythagoreans and others of the Near East, a number was considered to be the equivalent of the sum of the successive numbers from one to the designated number. For example, a certain wall etching reads, "I am in love with Harmony; the number of her darling name is forty-five." Van Eysinga indicates that the scribbler is confessing his love for music, the number (or symbol) of which was nine, since the numbers one through nine added equal forty-five.[22] Adopting this procedure, which must have been used rather frequently in the ancient world, 666 may be thus rendered: 666 is the sum of numbers from 1 to 36, while 36 is the sum of numbers to 8.[23] Revelation 17:11 offers further insight to the interpretation of the "eight": "As for the beast (antichrist) that was and is not, it is an eighth. . . ."

According to the apocalyptic background of the seer, the number six was considered a profane and incomplete number in contrast with the sacred and complete number seven. Considered from this aspect, three sixes (666) indicate absolute imperfection. Furthermore, in this manner the unclean six is tied closely to the number eight, which in many gnostic circles was used as an all-inclusive number to depict the entire realm of existence, the world and the powers surrounding it, including the heavenly world. Hence, 666 is taken by the seer to depict the gnostic's "human" caricature of Christ (that is, the gnostic docetic Christ) as the absolute in imperfection; while the number eight (17:11) is intended to identify the antichrist in his "demonic" perspective as originating from the gnostic "Wisdom." Thus this passage declares the author's recognition that the antichrist cannot be separated from his connection with false wisdom, any more than the true Christ can be severed from the "Wisdom of God." Revelation 13:18 then signifies that the one who is truly spiritual, who possesses true "Wisdom

from above," will be able to discern the error of the gnostic
doctrine of Christ and avoid its ruin.

The second beast (13:11-17), identified as the false
prophet of the first beast (16:13; 19:20; 20:10), is to be
understood collectively. It is the task of the false prophet
to disseminate the teachings connected with the antichrist
(13:12-17). Outwardly the false prophets may appear to
be members of the Christian community, but inwardly they
are inspired by the power of evil: ". . . it had two horns like
a lamb and it spoke like a dragon" (13:11). Moreover, these
false prophets are to be identified with the "many antichrists" of 1 John, as well as with the errorists of Jude and
2 Peter. In 2 Peter the heretics have the name of Balaam, as
in Revelation. Jude maintains that they walk after the
likeness of Cain, and he, too, mentions the sin of Balaam
and Korah. In 1 John these prophets are inspired by the
antichrist, and there is a reference to Cain, the only proper
name in his letter except Jesus.[24]

14:1 Then I looked, and lo, on Mount Zion stood the Lamb,
and with him a hundred and forty-four thousand who had his
name and his Father's name written on their foreheads. [2] And I
heard a voice from heaven like the sound of many waters and like
the sound of loud thunder; the voice I heard was like the sound
of harpers playing on their harps, [3] and they sing a new song before the throne and before the four living creatures and before the
elders. No one could learn that song except the hundred and forty-
four thousand who had been redeemed from the earth. [4] It is these
who have not defiled themselves with women, for they are chaste;
it is these who follow the Lamb wherever he goes; these have been
redeemed from mankind as first fruits for God and the Lamb,
[5] and in their mouth no lie was found, for they are spotless.

6 Then I saw another angel flying in midheaven, with an eternal
gospel to proclaim to those who dwell on earth, to every nation
and tribe and tongue and people; [7] and he said with a loud voice,
"Fear God and give him glory, for the hour of his judgment has
come; and worship him who made heaven and earth, the sea and
the fountains of water."

8 Another angel, a second, followed, saying, "Fallen, fallen is

Babylon the great, she who made all nations drink the wine of her impure passion."

9 And another angel, a third, followed them, saying with a loud voice, "If any one worships the beast and its image, and receives a mark on his forehead or on his hand, [10] he also shall drink the wine of God's wrath, poured unmixed into the cup of his anger, and he shall be tormented with fire and brimstone in the presence of the holy angels and in the presence of the Lamb. [11] And the smoke of their torment goes up for ever and ever; and they have no rest, day or night, these worshipers of the beast and its image, and whoever receives the mark of its name."

12 Here is a call for the endurance of the saints, those who keep the commandments of God and the faith of Jesus.

13 And I heard a voice from heaven saying, "Write this: Blessed are the dead who die in the Lord henceforth." "Blessed indeed," says the Spirit, "that they may rest from their labors, for their deeds follow them!"

14 Then I looked, and lo, a white cloud, and seated on the cloud one like a son of man, with a golden crown on his head, and a sharp sickle in his hand. [15] And another angel came out of the temple, calling with a loud voice to him who sat upon the cloud, "Put in your sickle, and reap, for the hour to reap has come, for the harvest of the earth is fully ripe." [16] So he who sat upon the cloud swung his sickle on the earth, and the earth was reaped.

17 And another angel came out of the temple in heaven, and he too had a sharp sickle. [18] Then another angel came out from the altar, the angel who has power over fire, and he called with a loud voice to him who had the sharp sickle, "Put in your sickle, and gather the clusters of the vine of the earth, for its grapes are ripe." [19] So the angel swung his sickle on the earth and gathered the vintage of the earth, and threw it into the great wine press of the wrath of God; [20] and the wine press was trodden outside the city, and blood flowed from the wine press, as high as a horse's bridle, for one thousand six hundred stadia.

The twelfth chapter of Revelation describes the appearance of the Redeemer, and the fourteenth delineates the results of his earthly descent. Among the gnostics it was believed that the Redeemer would descend to the earth and reveal to the elect the sacred mysteries of salvation, thus equipping them for their heavenward journey back to the world of light. This belief, known as the "Redeemer myth," was present in a multiplicity of forms, though all its presentations were guided by the same essential elements, all of which are reflected in the themes of Revelation 14, as well as in the underlying framework of Chapters 12-21.

By his use of this gnostic mythological pattern, John seems to be saying that the Redeemer has indeed made his appearance; but the gnostics, who pride themselves on their spiritual insights, are not able to recognize him. Chapter 14 might then be outlined: (1) the revelation of the Redeemer and the consequent recognition of him by those who have not had their garments defiled by the antinomian gnostic heresy (1-5); (2) the incapacity of the gnostic errorists to recognize and respond to the revelation of the Redeemer (6-13); and (3) the believer's assurance of final victory over all demonic foes (14-20).

The first division of Chapter 14 is the repetition of a theme alluded to in an earlier chapter (5:6 ff.). John chooses to use again his favorite term, Lamb, in the same manner that he used it in that previous passage. With no forewarning or preparation the Lamb suddenly appears from nowhere: "Then I looked, and lo, on Mount Zion stood the Lamb" (14:1). Appearing with him is a massive crowd, described in a multiple of a sacred number, 144,000. Concerning the large mass of people, John states that they sing a "new song" which no one can learn except those who have been redeemed from the earth, and they have his name and the Father's name inscribed upon their foreheads (14:3, 1b). Evidently the seer has used the common gnostic affirmation that only the redeemed will be able to recognize the Redeemer when he comes to reveal himself to the "spiritual" and to lead them back to the Father. To these he will impart a saving knowledge *(gnosis)* that will guide them to the Father. A section from a hymn of the Naasenes speaks of the impartation of this *gnosis:*

On this account, O Father, send me;
Bearing seals, I shall descend;
Through ages whole I'll sweep,
All mysteries I'll unravel,
And forms of Gods I'll show;
And secrets of the saintly path,
Styled "Gnosis," I'll impart (Hippolytus, V, V.).

Through the intentional conjunction of the Lamb concept with the Redeemer motif the seer has sought to refute an error which would separate the "spiritual Christ" from the earthly and physical Jesus. Though the emphasis may be upon the *victory* and *power* of the Lamb in Revelation, nevertheless any Christian reader would immediately associate this power with the *death* of his Lord. For John the impartation of *gnosis* to the elect must come through a Christ who has gained this power through his death; no impassive Christ who descends upon Jesus and then reascends before the passion is capable of this task. Any Christ of this sort would be simply a caricature of the true Redeemer, a demonic "beast."

The seer emphasizes two negative qualities which further describe those who possess the capacity to recognize the true Christ and to distinguish him from the pseudo-Christ of the gnostic theology. These have not defiled themselves with women, and nothing false is to be found in their mouths (14:4-5). The combination of these traits intimates that John is facing a libertine gnosticism which shares a false understanding of Christ. When one recalls the stringent opposition that John makes earlier against the libertine gnostics, the mention of "defilement" must be understood as the condition of those who pursue the antinomian way of life of the gnostics. That they are also spoken of as "false" indicates that they have related themselves to the false, or docetic, Christ.

In positive stress the "true gnostic," the "orthodox" Christian, is a "virgin" who follows the Lamb wherever he leads. Again John has placed together several gnostic motifs to describe the followers of the true Christ. The overall context, plus the identification of these with the people of 7:4, and the metaphorical use of "virgin" in this passage, suggest that these people be understood, not in the specific sense as martyrs, but in a broader sense as obedient followers of the risen Lord. The reference to those "who have not defiled themselves with women" (14:4) is to be interpreted as meaning those who have avoided contact with the heathen sexual rites as adopted by the heretical groups (cf. 3:4).[25] The Christian must follow wherever the heavenly Redeemer leads him — he must follow the Lamb through his passion, death, and victory over death. On the one hand, this denies a docetic Christology and an antinomian way of life through the identification of the redeemed with those traits of the Redeemer's earthly life. On the other hand, it guarantees to them, in the familiar gnostic form, guidance by the Redeemer for the heavenly journey.

The second division of Revelation 14 relates in vivid imagery the inability of the gnostic to respond to the true God and Savior. The gnostic claims a special insight and frowns upon those who he feels do not share this power. John reverses the situation by demonstrating that a person who is truly spiritual will recognize the Savior sent from the One who made heaven and earth, the sea and the fountains of water (14:7); and this One is not only Creator and Judge, but Redeemer as well. For John it is not the "spiritual," but the "unspiritual" who fails to acknowledge the unity of Creator and Redeemer. As the true followers know the true Christ and have his name and their Father's name imprinted upon their foreheads, so the pseudo-believers worship the pseudo-Christ and have his mark upon them (14:9). These adherents of the pseudo-Christ belong to the false Wisdom, Babylon, whose fall is proleptically pro-claimed. The mention of Babylon and her impurity (cf. 2:14) in connection with the false Christ (14:8 ff.) is the method by which the seer attempts to define again the content of the gnostic error: It is of Jewish origin (Babylon= pseudo-Jerusalem=pseudo-Wisdom), antinomian, and it professes a false Christ, whom John understands to be the caricature of the real Christ who suffered and died.

In the same way that Babylon is "drunk," so are all who belong to the false Wisdom. The gnostic appeal is for men to be "awakened" from their "sleep," or else to be "sobered" from their "drunkeness." The seer applies this exhortation in turn to those gnostics who refuse to keep the com-mandments of God and the faith of Jesus (14:12). He would agree with the gnostic Gospel of Thomas:

> Jesus said:
> "I stood in the midst of the world and
> I appeared to them in flesh;
> I found them all drunken;
> I found none among them thirsty.
> And my soul was pained for the children of men;
> for they are blind in their hearts,
> and they do not see
> that they came empty into the world
> seeking also to leave the world empty.
> But now they are drunken.
> When they throw off their wine,
> then they will repent." [26]

The final division of Revelation 14 deals with the presen-tation of certain victory to the followers of the Redeemer-Lamb. The gnostic assurance of final conquest over all foes is transferred to the crowd which follows the Lamb wherever he leads. This assurance of victory is demon-strated by the indication of destruction for all the foes of God's people (14:17-20) and by the gathering together of God's elect (14:14-16).

4. *Christ and the Consummation of History (15:1 — 22:5)*

A. GOD'S JUDGMENT AND THE CONSUMMATION (15:1 — 21:1)

These chapters are united through the theme of the judgment of God which falls upon both the world of men and of demons who have rebelled against God. In the same fashion as the previous plagues were preceded by an act of worship (4:1 — 5:14), so these final plagues (16:1-21) follow a worship experience (15:1-8). But whereas the earlier plagues pointed to God's judgment throughout the course of human history, the bowl-visions portray the final revelation of God's judgment by which history is brought to its consummation. That these visions are symbolic of God's *final* judgment upon the sin of the world is indicated by at least two factors: (1) the completeness of their effects as compared with the partial force of the other plagues; and (2) the observation that these visions culminate in the final overthrow of the world: "the cities of the nations fell. . . . And every island fled away, and no mountains were to be found" (16:19, 20).

15:1 Then I saw another portent in heaven, great and wonderful, seven angels with seven plagues, which are the last, for with them the wrath of God is ended.

2 And I saw what appeared to be a sea of glass mingled with fire, and those who had conquered the beast and its image and the number of its name, standing beside the sea of glass with harps of God in their hands. ³ And they sing the song of Moses, the servant of God, and the song of the Lamb, saying,

"Great and wonderful are thy deeds,

O Lord God the Almighty!

Just and true are thy ways,

O King of the ages!

⁴ Who shall not fear and glorify thy name, O Lord?

For thou alone art holy.

All nations shall come and worship thee,

for thy judgments have been revealed."

5 After this I looked, and the temple of the tent of witness in

heaven was opened, ⁶ and out of the temple came the seven angels with the seven plagues, robed in pure bright linen, and their breasts girded with golden girdles. ⁷ And one of the four living creatures gave the seven angels seven golden bowls full of the wrath of God who lives for ever and ever; ⁸ and the temple was filled with smoke from the glory of God and from his power, and no one could enter the temple until the seven plagues of the seven angels were ended.

16:1 Then I heard a loud voice from the temple telling the seven angels, "Go and pour out on the earth the seven bowls of the wrath of God."

2 So the first angel went and poured his bowl on the earth, and foul and evil sores came upon the men who bore the mark of the beast and worshiped its image.

3 The second angel poured his bowl into the sea, and it became like the blood of a dead man, and every living thing died that was in the sea.

4 The third angel poured his bowl into the rivers and the fountains of water, and they became blood. ⁵ And I heard the angel of water say,

"Just art thou in these thy judgments,
thou who art and wast, O Holy One.
⁶ For men have shed the blood of saints and prophets,
and thou hast given them blood to drink.
It is their due!"
⁷ And I heard the altar cry,
"Yea, Lord God the Almighty,
true and just are thy judgments!"

8 The fourth angel poured his bowl on the sun, and it was allowed to scorch men with fire; ⁹ men were scorched by the fierce heat, and they cursed the name of God who had power over these plagues, and they did not repent and give him glory.

10 The fifth angel poured his bowl on the throne of the beast, and its kingdom was in darkness; men gnawed their tongues in anguish ¹¹ and cursed the God of heaven for their pain and sores, and did not repent of their deeds.

12 The sixth angel poured his bowl on the great river Euphrates, and its water was dried up, to prepare the way for the kings from the east. ¹³ And I saw, issuing from the mouth of the dragon and from the mouth of the beast and from the mouth of the false prophet, three foul spirits like frogs; ¹⁴ for they are demonic spirits performing signs, who go abroad to the kings of the whole world, to assemble them for battle on the great day of God the Almighty. ¹⁵ ("Lo, I am coming like a thief! Blessed is he who is awake, keeping his garments that he may not go naked and be seen ex-

posed!") [16] And they assembled them at the place which is called in Hebrew Armageddon.

17 The seventh angel poured his bowl into the air, and a great voice came out of the temple, from the throne, saying, "It is done!" [18] And there were flashes of lightning, loud noises, peals of thunder, and a great earthquake such as had never been since men were on the earth, so great was that earthquake. [19] The great city was split into three parts, and the cities of the nations fell, and God remembered great Babylon, to make her drain the cup of the fury of his wrath. [20] And every island fled away, and no mountains were to be found; [21] and great hailstones, heavy as a hundredweight, dropped on men from heaven, till men cursed God for the plague of the hail, so fearful was that plague.

In anticipation of the final victory the people of God stand before his throne and sing the "song of Moses and the Lamb." This hymn commemorates God's judgment upon his foes, made possible through the mighty deeds of the Lamb, and calls to mind the earlier victory of God achieved in Egypt through Moses. Then with great solemnity the Temple is opened and the seven angels come forth bearing the golden bowls containing the seven final plagues of God's judgment upon the sinful world. These plagues prepare the way for the great act of redemption.

Once more can be seen the seer's orientation in the tradition of the Old Testament, for these seven bowl-plagues suggest events that took place in the course of the Exodus from Egypt. In particular, the first and third of the plagues follow rather closely two of the Egyptian plagues (Exodus 9:10; 7:20-21), while the Egyptian plague of turning the water into blood also becomes the basis for the second of the bowl-plagues. The fourth of the bowl-plagues, in which the heat of the sun is intensified, has its counterpart in the plague of darkness on Egypt, since both plagues are dependent upon the power of God over the sun. The drying up of the waters recalls what happened when Israel crossed the Red Sea (Exodus 14:21); and the seventh plague with its thunder, lightning, and hail perhaps has its basis in the events mentioned in Exodus 9:23-25.

Detailed explanation of each of these bowl-plagues is unnecessary, since they are so closely related to the trumpet-plagues, which have already been discussed. The primary difference between them is the completeness of the bowl-plagues as compared with the partial effect (on "one third") of the trumpet-plagues. However, the sixth in this series presents a unique element which requires some explanation. The sixth plague reflects Jewish and early Christian apocalyptic beliefs, according to which it was expected that at the end of time all the enemies of God would gather together for one final rebellious assault against God's people.

John states that this last battle will occur at a place called, in Hebrew, "Armageddon." It is highly probable that this name comes from the two Hebrew words meaning Mount Megiddo, for it was in the vicinity of this mountain that Israel won one of its most noted victories (Judges 5:19), and it was here also that many other battles were fought in Israel's early history. Perhaps in the circle of John's readers this name had been woven into certain apocalyptic myths, and in these was used to describe the place where God would win his final victory in the same fashion as it is used in the book of Revelation. After his final conquest over all earthly foes, God turns his judgment upon Babylon, the demonic force lying behind all evil on the earth (17:1 – 18:24).

17:1 Then one of the seven angels who had the seven bowls came and said to me, "Come, I will show you the judgment of the great harlot who is seated upon many waters, ² with whom the kings of the earth have committed fornication, and with the wine of whose fornication the dwellers on earth have become drunk." ³ And he carried me away in the Spirit into a wilderness, and I saw a woman sitting on a scarlet beast which was full of blasphemous names, and it had seven heads and ten horns. ⁴ The

woman was arrayed in purple and scarlet, and bedecked with gold
and jewels and pearls, holding in her hand a golden cup full of
abominations and the impurities of her fornication; ⁵ and on her
forehead was written a name of mystery: "Babylon the great,
mother of harlots and of earth's abominations." ⁶ And I saw the
woman, drunk with the blood of the saints and the blood of the
martyrs of Jesus.

When I saw her I marveled greatly. ⁷ But the angel said to me,
"Why marvel? I will tell you the mystery of the woman, and of
the beast with seven heads and ten horns that carries her. ⁸ The
beast that you saw was, and is not, and is to ascend from the bottomless pit and go to perdition; and the dwellers on earth whose
names have not been written in the book of life from the foundation of the world, will marvel to behold the beast, because it was
and is not and is to come. ⁹ This calls for a mind with wisdom:
the seven heads are seven hills on which the woman is seated;
¹⁰ they are also seven kings, five of whom have fallen, one is, the
other has not yet come, and when he comes he must remain only a
little while. ¹¹ As for the beast that was and is not, it is an eighth
but it belongs to the seven, and it goes to perdition. ¹² And the
ten horns that you saw are ten kings who have not yet received
royal power, but they are to receive authority as kings for one
hour, together with the beast. ¹³ These are of one mind and give
over their power and authority to the beast; ¹⁴ they will make war
on the Lamb, and the Lamb will conquer them, for he is Lord of
lords and Kings of kings, and those with him are called and chosen
and faithful."

15 And he said to me, "The waters that you saw, where the
harlot is seated, are peoples and multitudes and nations and
tongues. ¹⁶ And the ten horns that you saw, they and the beast
will hate the harlot; they will make her desolate and naked, and
devour her flesh and burn her up with fire, ¹⁷ for God has put it
into their hearts to carry out his purpose by being of one mind and
giving over their royal power to the beast, until the words of God
shall be fulfilled. ¹⁸ And the woman that you saw is the great city
which has dominion over the kings of the earth."

Chapter 17, quite important in the overall construction
of Revelation, is often taken to be the clue for the interpretation of the remainder of the book. However, it would
seem that the difficult and enigmatic allusions in this chapter are best understood in light of the more evident antignostic polemic in Revelation 2 – 3 and elsewhere.

Customarily, the references to Babylon are thought to be the seer's parody on Rome; but this is doubtful for several reasons. Babylon necessarily is a demonic force of an otherworldly sort, as is learned through the observation that *all* earthly cities are destroyed before God's judgment falls upon Babylon (18:19-20). Moreover, the description of Babylon as a trade city (especially with oriental merchandise!) is inconsistent with the Rome theory. Rome was noted for many things, but never for its commerce. Finally, how could it be said that the people of God of both the Old and the New Testament eras died there? [27]

It is much more satisfactory to assume that the references to "kings" and "mountains," and especially to Babylon as a "woman," are mythological and cosmological terms applied to the supernatural foes of God, rather than to historical persons such as the Roman emperors, or to the geographical setting of Rome as a city upon seven hills. [28] The gnostics were much impressed by cosmological speculations, and apocalyptic literature was filled with the raw materials for this sort of speculation. If John had in mind to speak against the gnostics in his community, it is highly probable that he would have taken over some of these cosmological and mythological figures to affirm his position and to oppose theirs.

The same thing may be said regarding the use of numbers in this chapter. John uses a myth in which a demonic monster rebels against God; and the seven heads and ten horns are more naturally conceived of as a part of the original description of the mythical monster than as an attempt to depict the succession of Roman emperors (the seven heads) or to include the company of Persian satraps (the ten horns). John personifies these attributes of the original monster so as to make its demonic proportions more intense and its power more fearful. In apocalyptic circles the numbers seven and ten were in frequent use apart from any particular historical connections, and there is no need to seek for historical or geographical allusions at this point. Something similar may be affirmed for the number five. Many persons in the ancient world held five to be a significant number because it was symbolic of the supernatural power lying behind the five planets, which were thought to exercise control over the fate and destiny of man. In particular, certain gnostic groups were very much concerned about the movements of the heavenly bodies and wove their myths about them. Finally, the number eight was looked upon in some gnostic circles as an all inclusive number for the totality of all supernatural powers.

If, then, John states that five have already fallen, one is now present, and the last is coming to reign but for a short time, and if he declares that the beast, who is the "eighth," is about to appear and go into destruction, this is his way of informing his readers of the certain and imminent destruction of God's enemies. And the seer himself intimates that he is speaking to a Christian community which possesses "true *gnosis*," for in his interpretation of the mysterious woman he uses a gnostic formula: "This mystery is for those who possess insight and wisdom."

Following the translation of Revelation 18, further elaboration will be given to the hypothesis that the woman in it and in the preceding chapter is none other than the embodiment of the False Wisdom of the gnostic group opposed by John.

18:1 After this I saw another angel coming down from heaven, having great authority; and the earth was made bright with his splendor. ² And he called out with a mighty voice,
"Fallen, fallen is Babylon the great!
It has become a dwelling place of demons,
a haunt of every foul spirit,
a haunt of every foul and hateful bird;

³ for all nations have drunk the wine of her impure passion,
and the kings of the earth have committed fornication with her,
and the merchants of the earth have grown rich with the wealth
of her wantonness."
⁴ Then I heard another voice from heaven saying,
"Come out of her, my people,
lest you take part in her sins,
lest you share in her plagues;
⁵ for her sins are heaped high as heaven,
and God has remembered her iniquities.
⁶ Render to her as she herself has rendered,
and repay her double for her deeds;
mix a double draught for her in the cup she mixed.
⁷ As she glorified herself and played the wanton,
so give her a like measure of torment and mourning.
Since in her heart she says, 'A queen I sit,
I am no widow, mourning I shall never see,'
⁸ so shall her plagues come in a single day,
pestilence and mourning and famine,
and she shall be burned with fire;
for mighty is the Lord God who judges her."
9 And the kings of the earth, who committed fornication and
were wanton with her, will weep and wail over her when they see
the smoke of her burning; ¹⁰ they will stand far off, in fear of her
torment, and say,
"Alas! alas! thou great city, thou mighty city, Babylon!
In one hour has thy judgment come."
11 And the merchants of the earth weep and mourn for her,
since no one buys their cargo any more, ¹² cargo of gold, silver,
jewels and pearls, fine linen, purple, silk and scarlet, all kinds of
scented wood, all articles of ivory, all articles of costly wood,
bronze, iron and marble, ¹³ cinnamon, spice, incense, myrrh, frank-
incense, wine, oil, fine flour and wheat, cattle and sheep, horses
and chariots, and slaves, that is, human souls.
¹⁴ "The fruit for which thy soul longed has gone from thee,
and all thy dainties and thy splendor are lost to thee, never to
be found again!"
¹⁵ The merchants of these wares, who gained wealth from her, will
stand far off, in fear of her torment, weeping and mourning aloud,
¹⁶ "Alas, alas, for the great city that was clothed in fine linen, in
purple and scarlet,
bedecked with gold, with jewels, and with pearls!
¹⁷ In one hour all this wealth has been laid waste."
And all shipmasters and seafaring men, sailors and all whose

trade is on the sea, stood far off [18] and cried out as they saw the smoke of her burning,

"What city was like the great city?"

[19] And they threw dust on their heads, as they wept and mourned, crying out,

"Alas, alas, for the great city

where all who had ships at sea grew rich by her wealth!

In one hour she has been laid waste.

[20] Rejoice over her, O heaven,

O saints and apostles and prophets,

for God has given judgment for you against her!"

21 Then a mighty angel took up a stone like a great millstone and threw it into the sea, saying,

"So shall Babylon the great city, be thrown down with violence, and shall be found no more;

[22] and the sound of harpers ahd minstrels, of flute players and trumpeters,

shall be heard in thee no more;

and a craftsman of any craft shall be found in thee no more;

and the sound of the millstone

shall be heard in thee no more;

[23] and the light of a lamp shall shine in thee no more;

and the voice of bridegroom and bride shall be heard in thee no more;

for thy merchants were the great men of the earth, and all nations were deceived by thy sorcery.

[24] And in her was found the blood of prophets and of saints, and of all who have been slain on earth."

Babylon symbolizes the Wisdom of the World, the gnostic pseudo-wisdom, which deceives the entire world and for whom a supra-historical judgment awaits. As in Revelation 21 the Bride of the Lamb is decorated with all the heavenly glory, so this woman who sits upon the beast is displayed in all the riches of the earth. This intimates that the seer intends a conscious contrast between the woman of Chapter 12 and the woman of 17 – 18. The former woman is the Heavenly Wisdom through whom God sent the Redeemer into the world; the latter woman represents the seer's parody upon the gnostic Wisdom, the Wisdom of the World, which was ultimately responsible for the crucifixion of Christ. This pseudo-wisdom is also the "mother" of all gnostic antinomianism and the basis of their participation in the idolatrous feasts (cf. 17:5). And it may be that a further comparison is intended, especially if the seer had in mind an analogy like that of

Wisdom has built her house, she has set up her seven pillars.	A foolish woman is noisy; she is wanton and knows no shame.
She has slaughtered her beasts, she has mixed her wine, she has also set her table.	She sits at the door of her house, she takes a seat on the high places of the town,
She has sent out her maids to call from the highest places in the town,	calling to those who pass by, who are going straight on their way,
"Whoever is simple, let him turn in here!"	"Whoever is simple, let him turn in here!"
To him who is without sense she says,	And to him who is without sense she says,
"Come, eat of my bread and drink of the wine I have mixed.	"Stolen water is sweet, and bread eaten in secret is pleasant."
Leave simpleness, and live, and walk in the way of insight."	But he does not know that the dead are there, that her guests are in the depths of Sheol.
Proverbs 9:1-6	Proverbs 9:13-18

Apparently, John has made a similar comparison, only in a much more dramatic fashion. For him also the Wisdom of God is established upon "seven pillars," the Wisdom of the World upon "seven mountains" (17:9); the True Wisdom prepares her table and offers wine, as does the False Wisdom; through participation in the Divine Wisdom one becomes wise, while participation in the Demonic Wisdom leaves one void of understanding and ripe for judgment. So real is the demonic nature of this False Wisdom that it can be delineated only in symbolic terminology. And when God's judgments in history are completed, there will be a special judgment for this Demonic Wisdom, which is, John feels, the supreme source of difficulty in the Christian community. He warns the people of God to flee its influence, lest they, too, become swayed by its demonic force (18:4). Indeed, the False Wisdom along with its antichrist has already lost the battle; and the true believers, who alone possess the Spirit of God, are the ones to whom God has revealed this mystery!

19:1 After this I heard what seemed to be the mighty voice of a great multitude in heaven, crying,
"Hallelujah! Salvation and glory and power belong to our God,
² for his judgments are true and just;
he has judged the great harlot who corrupted the earth with her fornication,
and he has avenged on her the blood of his servants."
³ Once more they cried,
"Hallelujah! The smoke from her goes up for ever and ever."
⁴ And the twenty-four elders and the four living creatures fell down and worshiped God who is seated on the throne, saying, "Amen. Hallelujah!"
⁵ And from the throne came a voice crying,
"Praise our God, all you his servants,
you who fear him, small and great."
⁶ Then I heard what seemed to be the voice of a great multitude, like the sound of many waters and like the sound of mighty thunderpeals, crying,
"Hallelujah! For the Lord our God the Almighty reigns.
⁷ Let us rejoice and exult and give him the glory,
for the marriage of the Lamb has come, and his Bride has made herself ready;
⁸ it was granted her to be clothed with fine linen, bright and pure"—
for the fine linen is the righteous deeds of the saints.
9 And the angel said to me, "Write this: Blessed are those who are invited to the marriage supper of the Lamb." And he said to me, "These are true words of God." ¹⁰ Then I fell down at his feet to worship him, but he said to me, "You must not do that! I am a fellow servant with you and your brethren who hold the testimony of Jesus. Worship God." For the testimony of Jesus is the spirit of prophecy.
11 Then I saw heaven opened, and behold, a white horse! He

who sat upon it is called Faithful and True, and in righteousness he judges and makes war. [12] His eyes are like a flame of fire, and on his head are many diadems; and he has a name inscribed which no one knows but himself. [13] He is clad in a robe dipped in blood, and the name by which he is called is The Word of God. [14] And the armies of heaven, arrayed in fine linen, white and pure, followed him on white horses. [15] From his mouth issues a sharp sword with which to smite the nations, and he will rule them with a rod of iron; he will tread the wine press of the fury of the wrath of God the Almighty. [16] On his robe and on his thigh he has a name inscribed, King of kings and Lord of lords.

17 Then I saw an angel standing in the sun, and with a loud voice he called to all the birds that fly in midheaven, "Come, gather for the great supper of God, [18] to eat the flesh of kings, the flesh of captains, the flesh of mighty men, the flesh of horses and their riders, and the flesh of all men, both free and slave, both small and great." [19] And I saw the beast and the kings of the earth with their armies gathered to make war against him who sits upon the horse and against his army. [20] And the beast was captured, and with it the false prophet who in its presence had worked the signs by which he deceived those who had received the mark of the beast and those who worshiped its image. These two were thrown alive into the lake of fire that burns with brimstone. [21] And the rest were slain by the sword of him who sits upon the horse, the sword that issues from his mouth; and all the birds were gorged with their flesh.

Revelation 19 presents the penultimate stage in the eschatological drama. This chapter opens with two hymns, the one looking back to the accomplished victory (19:1-2), and the other anticipating the impending wedding of the Lamb (19:6-8). In 19:13 comes the crowning point of the chain of thought begun in Chapter 12 with the birth of the Word of God. Now characterized as a warrior, this Person is judicial and eschatological. His name, the Word of God, well chosen for this purpose, suits perfectly the eschatological setting. As the creative Word of God, Christ is supreme, not only over the heavenly hierarchies of angels, but also over the demonic foes he is about to encounter.

Several facets of this passage demand attention. The seer

relates that this One has a name written that no one understands except himself (19:12). This impenetrable name is
an indication of his surpassing strength; and "no one" must
be interpreted as the equivalent of "not one of the men
having the mark of the beast" (cf. 14:3b; 2:7; 5:5). John
thereby repeats his thesis, which he often brings to light,
that the gnostics do not and cannot know the true nature
of the Lord. The gnostic interpretation of Christ is so far
distant from the Christian viewpoint that his "name" remains hidden to them. On the other hand, the true believers recognize the Lord in his true perspective, and to
them he is Faithful and True, the Word of God.

The conquest of the Redeemer's enemies comes about by
a sharp sword coming forth from his mouth (19:15). Immediately there is a reminder of what was said in the letter
to the church at Pergamum, where those who were described as holding to the teachings of the Balaamites and
the Nicolaitans were present. John mentions no activity
on the part of the followers of the Word of God. The defeat of the antichrist, the false prophet, and their cohorts
comes about solely by the sword which proceeds from the
mouth of Christ. In an earlier passage the defeat of the
dragon is said to have been achieved through the blood
of the Lamb and the testimony of the redeemed (12:11).
Both passages must be taken together. The Christian
apocalyptist is contrasting the fate of the believers and the
gnostics with respect to their confession of the real passion
and death of the Lord. The same word which guides the
"spiritual" to the Father becomes the word which destroys
the "earthly" gnostic, because he denies a Christ who
empties his blood for salvation. This message is the sword
by which the antichrist is defeated.

20:1 Then I saw an angel coming down from heaven, holding

in his hand the key of the bottomless pit and a great chain. ² And he seized the dragon, that ancient serpent, who is the Devil and Satan, and bound him for a thousand years, ³ and threw him into the pit, and shut it and sealed it over him, that he should deceive the nations no more, till the thousand years were ended. After that he must be loosed for a little while.

4 Then I saw thrones, and seated on them were those to whom judgment was committed. Also I saw the souls of those who had been beheaded for their testimony to Jesus and for the word of God, and who had not worshiped the beast or its image and had not received its mark on their foreheads or their hands. They came to life, and reigned with Christ a thousand years. ⁵ The rest of the dead did not come to life until the thousand years were ended. This is the first resurrection. ⁶ Blessed and holy is he who shares in the first resurrection! Over such the second death has no power, but they shall be priests of God and of Christ, and they shall reign with him a thousand years.

7 And when the thousand years are ended, Satan will be loosed from his prison ⁸ and will come out to deceive the nations which are at the four corners of the earth, that is, Gog and Magog, to gather them for battle; their number is like the sand of the sea. ⁹ And they marched up over the broad earth and surrounded the camp of the saints and the beloved city; but fire came down from heaven and consumed them, ¹⁰ and the devil who had deceived them was thrown into the lake of fire and brimstone where the beast and the false prophet were, and they will be tormented day and night for ever and ever.

11 Then I saw a great white throne and him who sat upon it; from his presence earth and sky fled away, and no place was found for them. ¹² And I saw the dead, great and small, standing before the throne, and books were opened. Also another book was opened, which is the book of life. And the dead were judged by what was written in the books, by what they had done. ¹³ And the sea gave up the dead in it, Death and Hades gave up the dead in them, and all were judged by what they had done. ¹⁴ Then Death and Hades were thrown into the lake of fire. This is the second death, the lake of fire; ¹⁵ and if any one's name was not found written in the book of life, he was thrown into the lake of fire.

Revelation 20 is actually a continuation of the judgment begun in the chapter immediately preceding; the victory initiated by the Word of God is brought to its consummation. Into this chapter are woven together several myths common to other Jewish apocalyptic sources — myths which the seer uses to underline the message he desires to convey. As one reads the somewhat cryptic account in this chapter, he must remember that he is reading apocalyptic imagery, and so must not allow himself to become lost in the form and thereby miss the meaning conveyed by the imagery.

The overall purpose of this chapter of Revelation is two-fold: (1) to describe the special benefits to be bestowed upon those who have endured unto death for their witness to the Lord; and (2) to intensify the reality of the final judgment upon all who have rejected the purpose of God. The first of these is bound closely to the theme of the thousand-year reign; the second is intimately related to the motif of the final judgment and the lake of fire.

It seems best to understand the mention of the thousand-year reign as John's means of encouraging his readers to be faithful to the point of death, if necessary. In Jewish (and early Christian) thought there were many different view-points regarding the nature of the afterlife, and John unites two of the most frequent concepts. In some circles it was believed that the afterlife would be in the form of a glorified earthly existence in which the people of God would enjoy peace and prosperity such as had never been experienced on earth before. In other circles all hopes for fulfillment of life on this earth had been abandoned and hopes were directed toward a future heavenly existence. Furthermore, ever since the time of the Jewish revolt against the Syrian king, Antiochus Epiphanes (*ca.* 175 B.C.), when many of the faithful suffered martyrdom, it was believed that those who had died for their faith would have a special place in the coming kingdom, whether it be earthly or heavenly.

All these themes have been united in the description of a thousand-year reign; and it is significant that John promises the same special benefits, not only to those who had been martyred for their faith, but to all those who had refused to worship the beast or his image; that is, to all who had overcome the temptation of gnosticism.

One must not take too literally the mention of the thousand-year reign. This concept does not appear elsewhere in the New Testament, and it is mentioned only here in the book of Revelation. Arguments concerning how or when it will take place are beyond the seer's purpose, and certainly do not reflect the same spirit in which he wrote. Least complicated is the assumption that John intends these figures, not to be understood literally, but to be interpreted as parables to describe the glorious future which God has in store for his people.

The second aim of this chapter is to assure the readers of the certain overthrow and destruction of their enemies, who also are the enemies of God. Again, John uses figures current in other apocalyptic sources to make known the fate of all who rebel against the divine will. Along with the defeat of Satan and his cohorts is the final end of "Death and Hades," that is death and the grave, which are feared by all men, but which no longer have authority over the people of God who now await the arrival of Jerusalem from above.

B. god's grace and the consummation (21:1 – 22:5)

Not only is the judgment of God active upon the sins of rebellious mankind, but the grace of God is abundantly generous toward those who in faith have followed the Lamb. And it is the goal of this section to convey this truth.

21:1 Then I saw a new heaven and a new earth; for the first heaven and the first earth had passed away, and the sea was no more. [2] And I saw the holy city, new Jerusalem, coming down out of heaven from God, prepared as a bride adorned for her husband;

³ and I heard a great voice from the throne saying, "Behold, the dwelling of God is with men. He will dwell with them, and they shall be his people, and God himself will be with them; ⁴ he will wipe away every tear from their eyes, and death shall be no more, neither shall there be mourning nor crying nor pain any more, for the former things have passed away."

5 And he who sat upon the throne said, "Behold, I make all things new." Also he said, "Write this, for these words are trustworthy and true." ⁶ And he said to me, "It is done! I am the Alpha and the Omega, the beginning and the end. To the thirsty I will give water without price from the fountain of the water of life. ⁷ He who conquers shall have this heritage, and I will be his God and he shall be my son. ⁸ But as for the cowardly, the faithless, the polluted, as for murderers, fornicators, sorcerers, idolaters, and all liars, their lot shall be in the lake that burns with fire and brimstone, which is the second death."

9 Then came one of the seven angels who had the seven bowls full of the seven last plagues, and spoke to me, saying, "Come, I will show you the Bride, the wife of the Lamb." ¹⁰ And in the Spirit he carried me away to a great, high mountain, and showed me the holy city Jerusalem coming down out of heaven from God, ¹¹ having the glory of God, its radiance like a most rare jewel, like a jasper, clear as crystal. ¹² It had a great, high wall, with twelve gates, and at the gates twelve angels, and on the gates the names of the twelve tribes of the sons of Israel were inscribed; ¹³ on the east three gates, on the north three gates, on the south three gates, and on the west three gates. ¹⁴ And the wall of the city had twelve foundations, and on them the twelve names of the twelve apostles of the Lamb.

15 And he who talked to me had a measuring rod of gold to measure the city and its gates and walls. ¹⁶ The city lies foursquare, its length the same as its breadth; and he measured the city with his rod, twelve thousand stadia; its length and breadth and height are equal. ¹⁷ He also measured its wall, a hundred and forty-four cubits by a man's measure, that is, an angel's. ¹⁸ The wall was built of jasper, while the city was pure gold, clear as glass. ¹⁹ The foundations of the wall of the city were adorned with every jewel; the first was jasper, the second sapphire, the third agate, the fourth emerald, ²⁰ the fifth onyx, the sixth carnelian, the seventh chrysolite, the eighth beryl, the ninth topaz, the tenth chrysoprase, the eleventh jacinth, the twelfth amethyst. ²¹ And the twelve gates were twelve pearls, each of the gates made of a single pearl, and the street of the city was pure gold, transparent as glass.

22 And I saw no temple in the city, for its temple is the Lord God the Almighty and the Lamb. ²³ And the city has no need of

sun or moon to shine upon it, for the glory of God is its light, and its lamp is the Lamb. [24] By its light shall the nations walk; and the kings of the earth shall bring their glory into it, [25] and its gates shall never be shut by day — and there shall be no night there; [26] they shall bring into it the glory and the honor of the nations. [27] But nothing unclean shall enter it, nor any one who practices abomination or falsehood, but only those who are written in the Lamb's book of life.

22:1 Then he showed me the river of the water of life, bright as crystal, flowing from the throne of God and of the Lamb [2] through the middle of the street of the city; also, on either side of the river, the tree of life with its twelve kinds of fruit, yielding its fruit each month; and the leaves of the tree were for the healing of the nations. [3] There shall no more be anything accursed, but the throne of God and of the Lamb shall be in it, and his servants shall worship him; [4] they shall see his face, and his name shall be on their foreheads. [5] And night shall be no more; they need no light of lamp or sun, for the Lord God will be their light, and they shall reign for ever and ever.

Into this section of Revelation are woven together at least three themes: (1) the heavenly city, (2) the new Jerusalem, and (3) paradise. The concept of the heavenly city is not without its counterpart in the thought of other people; for example, the Babylonian belief in a heavenly Babel, while the notion of a new (perhaps, a renewed) Jerusalem is not foreign to Jewish apocalyptic thought. Finally, the belief in paradise (*e.g.*, the stream and the tree of life) was a transfer of the picture of the Garden of Eden to the coming age. The original condition of man's world would be recreated, this time never to be destroyed. One should notice in the overall picture how the apostle maintains the basic concepts of his faith, even in his description of this golden city. Although the city is adorned with all kinds of precious stones, the primary emphasis is not upon the richness of the surroundings, but upon the realization of that which truly constitutes heaven, the experience of God's immediate and eternal presence with his people (21:3).

Important for this study is not the origin of any of these concepts, but the purpose for which John uses them; and it seems quite likely that he uses them as a polemic against the gnostic movement. In the "hymn of the soul" in the gnostic Acts of Thomas, the account begins with the promise of the birth of a divine child and is consummated with the allusion to his wedding after he returns to his father. Accordingly, the seer begins his account in Chapter 12 with the birth of the divine child and climaxes it in Chapter 21 with the allusion to the wedding. And in this context the reference is no doubt polemical: The seer triumphs in the fact that it is not Babylon but Jerusalem who is the bride.[29] John's specific purpose in recording this last phase of the redemptive drama is to clarify who will be with the Father through the Redeemer. He affirms that no one who is connected with the Worldly Wisdom (Babylon) and its consequent antinomianism will be united with the Father; only those who accept the Wisdom from Above (Jerusalem), mediated through the Redeemer who has suffered and died, will participate in the wedding.

C. EPILOGUE (22:6-21)

The story has been told, the truth revealed, but in order to underline what has been made known to the seer, the Lord himself adds to the testimony of John.

22:6 And he said to me, "These words are trustworthy and true. And the Lord, the God of the spirits of the prophets, has sent his angel to show his servants what must soon take place. ⁷ And behold, I am coming soon."

Blessed is he who keeps the words of the prophecy of this book.

8 I John am he who heard and saw these things. And when I heard and saw them, I fell down to worship at the feet of the angel who showed them to me; ⁹ but he said to me, "You must not do that! I am a fellow servant with you and your brethren

the prophets, and with those who keep the words of this book. Worship God."

10 And he said to me, "Do not seal up the words of the prophecy of this book, for the time is near. [11] Let the evil-doer still do evil, and the filthy still be filthy, and the righteous still do right, and the holy still be holy."

12 "Behold, I am coming soon, bringing my recompense, to repay every one for what he has done. [13] I am the Alpha and the Omega, the first and the last, the beginning and the end."

14 Blessed are those who wash their robes, that they may have the right to the tree of life and that they may enter the city by the gates. [15] Outside are the dogs and sorcerers and fornicators and murderers and idolaters, and every one who loves and practices falsehood.

16 "I Jesus have sent my angel to you with this testimony for the churches. I am the root and the offspring of David, the bright morning star."

17 The Spirit and the Bride say, "Come." And let him who hears say, "Come." And let him who is thirsty come, let him who desires take the water of life without price.

18 I warn every one who hears the words of the prophecy of this book: if any one adds to them, God will add to him the plagues described in this book, [19] and if any one takes away from the words of the book of this prophecy, God will take away his share in the tree of life and in the holy city, which are described in this book.

20 He who testifies to these things says, "Surely I am coming soon." Amen. Come, Lord Jesus!

21 The grace of the Lord Jesus be with all the saints. Amen.

Two passages specifically forbid angel worship on the part of John (19:10; 22:8-9). It is possible that these passages are intended either to emphasize the prophetic rank of the seer or to place the angel and the prophet on the same level in the sight of God. But it is more likely that these prohibitions are inserted as a corrective to the veneration of angels by a gnostic sect. It is characteristic of the book of Revelation, as with other earlier Jewish apocalypses, that God is far distant. To span this gap, various orders of angels were introduced; and in gnostic thought angels were understood as powers or aeons that were emanations from the supreme God of Light. Paul himself was very definitely antiangelic; and we learn from him that angel worship was common in this region (*e.g.* Colossians 2:8-13; 1:15-20).

This really explains the inclusion of these two passages in Revelation. John is in combat with a sect of gnostics who have a tendency to venerate angels and who classify the Creator as one of the lower angels. Here the believer is warned to worship no angel, not even one who reveals to him the knowledge concerning cosmological and soteriological mysteries. He must worship the one true God, Creator of heaven and earth and Redeemer of the faithful.

summary
and
conclusions

It is important to draw together some of the conclusions of the previous chapters and to look at the significance of the book as a whole.

What is customarily known as the contemporary-historical approach has been pursued in the interpretation of Revelation; for it is axiomatic that any book of the New Testament must be understood in light of its particular historical situation. The proponents of the contemporary-historical method of interpretation acknowledge the relevance of the book of Revelation for all generations of believers; but they also recognize that its relevance for the contemporary community of faith must come from the truths that the author intended to give to the people of his own day. In its usual form this view maintains that Revelation depicts the conflict of the early church with the political-religious strength of the Roman Empire. Babylon is equated with Rome; the first beast represents the emperor-cult; the second beast its priesthood; and the seven heads of the beasts stand for Roman emperors.

On the basis of the foregoing discussion, it appears that the background of a political persecution was not the original context for the writing of Revelation. Persecution was always a possibility after the destruction of Jerusalem, yet no specific signs of a general persecution are reflected either in Revelation or in any other New Testament book. *The historical setting of Revelation must be sought in the conflict of ideologies: Christianity in a life-death struggle with the gnostic perversion of the Christian faith.*

Significance of the Letters in Revelation 2 – 3

It has been suggested, in connection with the discussion of the letters to the seven churches, that the solution of the perplexing problem pertaining to the selection of these particular churches is determined by a *theological* purpose. The seer addresses himself to those communities in which he feels he may still have an influence in their ecclesiastical affairs. To these churches he writes with encouragement and rebuke so that they might be guided away from the dangers of the gnostic heresy.

The problem faced in Revelation 2 – 3 is manifestly a Jewish gnostic problem. Political conflicts are impossible to substantiate. This recognition has served as a canon of interpretation for the more difficult sections of Revelation. It has seemed logical to seek the meaning of the challenging and mysterious imagery in the remainder of Revelation in light of the evident foes of Christ and his church as they are pictured in these chapters. Otherwise, there is no real coherence and unity between the content of the letters and the remainder of Revelation. In the letters the seer describes the effects of the gnostic heresy upon the church; afterwards he proceeds to depict through symbolic imagery the ungodly force that has set into motion this distortion of the faith.

The Gnostic Problem and Polemic in Revelation

Gnostic sources later than the date of Revelation have

been used, inasmuch as no original gnostic sources from the time of Revelation are extant. It is acknowledged that all elements in the later gnostic sects were most certainly not present in the initial stages of the movement, yet several factors must be called to mind. (1) The gnostic sects of the second century do not arrive "full blown," but are developments from earlier groups. (2) All the gnostic sects known express the *same basic philosophy*, which determines their way of life. That is, the basic presuppositions are present in all the sects, regardless of the particular myths peculiar to any given sect — *dualism, redemption* for the spiritual through the possession of *gnosis*, and *freedom* with respect to lowly fleshly substance of the body. (3) The later sects reflect not only the basic gnostic presuppositions, but also certain of the *symbols* and *terminology* which were present at the earlier stage, though the meaning of these symbols and terms may have been altered. The book of Revelation shares many of these concepts — serpent deity, Wisdom, book of life, mysterious use of numbers, secret formulas, Redeemer myth, and the wedding theme. (4) The recently discovered gnostic sources have tended to confirm the accuracy of Irenaeus and Hippolytus in their works against heresy. And so, one will not go far astray in using these later writings to characterize some of the earlier movements.

The gnostic influence opposed by Revelation seems to have come into the churches through the medium of a Judaism which had embraced gnosticism. *Certainly, primitive Christian gnosticism had its forerunner in Judaism.* There can be no doubt that the Christian gnostic sects, such as the Sethians, the Cainites, and the Baruch gnostics of Justin, were purely Jewish and venerated a hero from Jewish history as a redeemer. The Jews as the source of gnosticism were opposed not only in Corinth, but also perhaps in Colossae (Colossians 2:16), and certainly in the Pastorals (Titus 1:10, 14; 1 Timothy 1:7). By his use of the term "Judaism," Ignatius, too, fights the gnostics.[1]

A similar decision must be made with regard to Revelation, which quite clearly identifies the enemies of the Christian community as one: Jewish gnostics. In particular there appear to be especially close analogies between the later Ophites and the sect opposed by the author of Revelation, and attention has been given to this hypothesis in certain passages. Evidently the later Ophites differed in some respects from the group which the seer confronts (as one would expect a group to change), but it appears that an earlier stage of at least a related system is the main movement opposed in Revelation.

As was mentioned previously, the author of Revelation chose the apocalyptic method for his writing because the gnostics themselves were given to myths. But beyond this, the myth is more serviceable than any other form of literature to express the demonic dimensions of the heretical sect and the certainty of God's triumph; and the relation of the myth to the historical person of Jesus Christ affirms that the Christian faith is a truly historical religion, as opposed to the empty speculations of gnosticism.

One final observation. The fact that Revelation is antignostic may have been the ultimate reason for its having been incorporated into the New Testament canon in place of several other apocalypses that were considered. It may well be, too, as some have suggested, that the gnostic polemic of James is the cause for its inclusion in the canon, as seems to have been the case with 2 Peter and the book of Acts. Second Peter is accepted, while the Gospel of Peter, with its docetic tendencies, is rejected; the Pastorals are included, though the gnostic-tainted Acts of Paul is refused. Perhaps the reason for the inclusion of the Revelation (of John), rather than the Revelation of Peter — its arch rival for canonicity — is due primarily to the antignostic elements in the former that are lacking in the latter.[2]

The Contemporary Value of Revelation

The dangers of gnosticism are ever present with the church — the one-sided interest in the deity of our Lord to the exclusion of his genuine humanity, the failure to understand history as the working-out of God's purpose despite the rebellion of mankind, the misinterpretation and misuse of Christian liberty, and the interest in "saving a man's soul" rather than concern for him as a total being. These are a few of the most obvious indications in the contemporary church of a gnostic influence akin to that opposed by Revelation. The seer calls us away from these distortions of our faith as much today as in his own time.

But the most dynamic value of Revelation is not what it has to say in the negative; its greatest contribution is positive. Nowhere else do we encounter so dramatically the affirmation that the one God, who in the beginning created the world, who at one unique moment in history revealed the mystery of salvation to the world through his Son, and who presently sustains the world, is the same God who at the end of history will declare the eternal destiny of all men. Indeed, this is the faith that empowers the believer to be "faithful unto death"; for he knows that "the kingdom of the world has become the kingdom of our Lord and of his Christ, and he shall reign for ever and ever" (11:15).

notes

Chapter One

[1] This chapter is based on the author's article, "The Fallacy of the Domitian Hypothesis," *New Testament Studies*, X (October, 1963), pp. 133-139.

[2] For a history of the interpretation of Revelation see the following: W. Bousset, *Die Offenbarung Johannis* (Göttingen: Vandenhoeck und Ruprecht, 1906), pp. 49-119; Theodor Zahn, *Die Offenbarung des Johannes* (third edition; Leipzig: A. Deichert'sche Verlagsbuchhandlung; Dr. Werner Scholl, 1924), I, pp. 54-100; R. H. Charles, *The Revelation of St. John* in *The International Critical Commentary* (New York: Charles Scribner's Sons, 1920), Vol. I, pp. clxxxiii-clxxxviii; I. T. Beckwith, *The Apocalypse of John* (New York: The Macmillan Company, 1919), pp. 318-336; E. Lohmeyer, "Die Offenbarung des Johannes 1920-1934," *Theologische Rundshau*, VI (1934), pp. 269-314; *idem*, VII (1935), pp. 28-62.

[3] Martin Rist, *The Revelation of St. John the Divine* in *The Interpreter's Bible*, George Arthur Buttrick (ed.) (Nashville: Abingdon Press, 1957), Vol. XII, p. 354.

[4] E. Lohmeyer, *op. cit.*, VI (1934), p. 284.

[5] For a discussion of the terms *gnosis* and *gnosticism*, see the third chapter.

[6] *E.g.* Williston Walker, *A History of the Christian Church* (New York: Charles Scribner's Sons, 1950), p. 34, "Of this persecution under Domitian (81-96) few details are known, but it must have been of severity in Rome and Asia Minor." For support of this theory of a Domitian persecution he appeals to 1 Clement 1, Rev. 2:10, 7:13, 14, in *loc. cit.*, fn. 5.

[7] Alexander Roberts and James Donaldson (eds.), *The Apostolic Fathers with Justin Martyr and Irenaeus* in *The Ante-Nicene Fathers* (American reprint of the Edinburgh edition, revised and chronologically arranged with brief notes and prefaces by A. Cleveland Coxe),

115

10 vols. (Grand Rapids: Wm. B. Eerdmans Publishing Co., 1951), Vol. I, p. 559, fn. 5.

[8] Eusebius *The Ecclesiastical History* III, xviii. 1-4, trans. Kirsopp Lake (New York: G. P. Putnam's Sons, 1926), © by G. P. Putnam's Sons, Vol. I, p. 235.

[9] Morton Scott Enslin, *Christian Beginnings* (New York: Harper & Row, Publishers, 1938), p. 365.

[10] 1 Enoch 21:3-6, *The Book of Enoch*, R. H. Charles (ed.) (Oxford: Clarendon Press, 1893), pp. 44-45.

[11] The only really significant examinations of Revelation in light of the possibility that it is an antignostic document have been made by van den Bergh van Eysinga in two articles, "Die in der Apocalypse bekampfte Gnosis," *Zeitschrift für Neutestamentliche Wissenschaft (ZNTW)*, XIII (1912), pp. 293-305; "Symbolisches in die Apokalypse Johannes," AO, II (1922), pp. 32-38; and Phillip Carrington, *The Meaning of the Revelation* (London: Society for the Promotion of Christian Knowledge, 1931), Appendix II, pp. 395-416.

Chapter Two

[1] Eduard Schick, *Die Apocalypse* in *Die Heilige Schrift in Deutscher Ubersetzung. Das Neue Testament*, Karl Staab (ed.) Wurzburg: Ecter-Verlag, 1952), p. 15; Martin Kiddle and M. K. Ross, *The Revelation of St. John* in *The Moffatt New Testament Commentary.* (New York: Harper & Row, Publishers, 1940), pp. 18, 5, 6.

[2] Ernst Lohmeyer, *Die Offenbarung des Johannes.* (Band XVI of *Handbuch zum Neuen Testament)* Gunther Bornkamm (ed.) (second edition; Tübingen: J. C. B. Mohr [Paul Siebeck], 1953), p. 43.

[3] Joseph Könn, *Gott und Satan* (Koln: Benziger Verlag, 1949), p. 58.

[4] W. M. Ramsay, *The Letters to the Seven Churches of Asia* (London: Hodder & Stoughton, n.d.), p. 191.

[5] *Ibid.*, pp. 191-192.

[6] Walter Bauer, *Rechtgläubigkeit und Ketzerei im Altesten Christentum* (Tübingen: Verlag von J. C. B. Mohr [Paul Siebeck], 1934), p. 82.

[7] James Moffatt, *Introduction to the Literature of the New Testament* (New York: Charles Scribner's Sons, 1927), p. 327.

[8] F. J. A. Hort, *The First Epistle of St. Peter 1:1 — 2:17* (London: Macmillan, 1898), pp. 17, 157-184. In this he is followed by Moffatt, *op. cit.,* p. 327; *idem, The General Epistles, The Moffatt New Testament Commentary* (New York: Harper & Row, Publishers, n. d.), p. 86; E. G. Selwyn, *The First Epistle of St. Peter* (London: Macmillan and Co., Ltd., 1949), pp. 119, 45-47.

[9] Hans Windisch, *Die Katholischen Briefe* (third edition; Tübing-

en: Verlag J. C. B. Mohr [Paul Siebeck], 1951), p. 51. D. G. Wohlenberg, *Der Erste und Zweite Petrusbrief und der Judasbrief* (Leipzig: A. Diechert'sche Verlagsbuchhandlung Werner Scholl, 1915), pp. xv, 3, 4, expresses almost the exact view that Windisch presents in his discussion.

[10] Bauer, *op. cit.*, pp. 83 ff.

[11] Ignatius, *Ephesians*, 9, *Early Christian Fathers*, Cyril Richardson (ed.) (Philadelphia: Westminster Press, 1953), p. 90.

[12] Eusebius *The Ecclesiastical History* III. xxxi. *op. cit.*, p. 271.

Chapter Three

[1] R. McL. Wilson, *The Gnostic Problem, A Study of the Relations Between Hellenistic Judaism and the Gnostic Heresy* (London: A. R. Mowbray and Co., 1958), p. 65.

[2] For a history of the study of gnosticism which reveals the multiplicity of ways in which the term has been used, cf. Hans Jonas, *Gnosis und Spätantiker Geist* (2 vols.; Göttingen: Vandenhoeck und Ruprecht, 1934), Vol. I, pp. 1-91.

[3] Rudolf Bultmann, *Primitive Christianity in Its Contemporary Setting*, trans. R. H. Fuller (New York: Meridian Books, 1956), p. 162.

[4] *Ibid.* Cf. *idem*, *Theology of the New Testament*, trans. Kendrick Gobel (2 vols.; New York: Charles Scribner's Sons, 1951-1955), Vol. I, p. 165, where he states, ". . . the essence of Gnosticism does not lie in its syncretistic mythology but rather in a new understanding — new in the ancient world — of man and the world; its mythology is only the expression of this understanding."

[5] Wilson, *op. cit.*, p. 69.

[6] Cf. Hans Liesegang, *Die Gnosis* (Stuttgart: Alfred Kröner Verlag, 1955), p. 5, who describes gnosticism as a mosaic; Carl Schneider, *Geitesgeschichte des Antiken Christentums* (2 vols.; München: C. H. Beck'sche Verlagsbuchhandlung, 1954), Vol. I, p. 270, concludes that there is no "Urform" of gnosis, but it is rather an eclectic movement which is able to absorb and to unite diverse elements; Hans Lietzman, *The Beginnings of the Christian Church*, Vol. I of *A History of the Early Church*, trans. Bertram Lee Woolf (Cleveland: Meridian Books, The World Publishing Company, 1953), Vol. I, p. 277, takes a related viewpoint; while B. J. Kidd, *A History of the Church* (3 vols.; Oxford: Clarendon Press, 1922), Vol. I, p. 193, states "[gnosticism] was rooted in syncretism."

[7] C. H. Dodd, *The Interpretation of the Fourth Gospel* (Cambridge: University Press, 1954), p. 97; Wilson, *op. cit.*, p. 68.

[8] Gilles Quispel, *Gnosis als Weltreligion* (Zurich: Origo Verlag, 1951), p. 29.

[9] *Ibid.* Cf. Alfred Loisy, *The Birth of the Christian Religion*, trans.

L. P. Jacks (London: George Allen and Unwin Ltd., 1948), p. 296, "The doctrine it proclaimed was a mystical knowledge of the divine secret and of the revealed programme of salvation."

[10] Liesegang, *op. cit.*, p. 1; Walter Schmithals, *Die Gnosis in Korinth. Eine Untersuchung zu den Korintherbriefen* (Göttingen: Vandenhoeck und Ruprecht, 1956), p. 65, states this is the classic formulation of gnosis.

[11] Wilson, *op. cit.*, p. 207; Bultmann, *Christianity*, pp. 163 ff.; *idem, Theol.*, Vol. I, p. 165.

[12] Bultmann, *Theol.*, Vol. I, p. 165. Cf. Jonas, *op. cit.*, Vol. I, pp. 96-98; Jonas, *op. cit.*, Vol. I, pp. 141 ff., emphasizes the "at-homeness" of the Greek in the world as opposed to the feeling of the gnostic.

[13] Bultmann, *Christianity*, p. 164.

[14] Bultmann, *Theol.*, Vol. I, p. 165.

[15] Bultmann, *Christianity*, p. 166, points out "the anthropology of Gnosticism is . . . trichotomous. It distinguishes body, soul, and Self."

[16] Schneider, *op. cit.*, Vol. I, p. 281.

[17] Quispel, *op. cit.*, pp. 42, 43. Quispel alludes to Valentinus' concept of Wisdom's fate as quoted in Irenaeus I. xxx. 3, "She was bound by a material body and very much burdened, she *came to herself*, and sought to flee from the waters of chaos and ascend again to the Mother in the Pleroma." In this Quispel points out that the coming-to-herself and the ascending are bound together.

[18] Bultmann, *Primitive Christianity*, p. 168.

[19] Bultmann, *Theol.*, I, p. 168, notes the difference between the New Testament emphasis upon the resurrection from the dead coupled with the notion of a final judgment as opposed to the gnostic teaching of the heavenly journey of the self.

[20] Schmithals, *op. cit.*, p. 65.

[21] *Ibid.*, p. 67.

[22] Schneider, *op. cit.*, I, p. 282.

[23] Irenaeus I. xxi. 5, in Schneider, *loc. cit.*

[24] Quispel, *op. cit.*, p. 34; cf. Liesegang, *op. cit.*, p. 24.

[25] Wilson, *op. cit.*, p. 203.

[26] Cf. Henry Longueville Mansel, *The Gnostic Heresies of the First and Second Centuries* (London: John Murray, 1875), pp. 82-84. Helena is understood as the first Conception of Simon's mind by whom he conceived the thought of making the angels and archangels. This conception proceeded from him and descended to the lower world and produced the angels and powers who in turn made the present world. Note Irenaeus I. xxiii. 2, "For this Ennoia leaping forth from him, and comprehending the will of her father, descended to the lower regions (of space), and generated angels and powers, by whom also he declared this world was formed."

[27] Mansel, *op. cit.*, pp. 167-168, believes the first theory of Valen-

tinus concerning the origin of the world can be traced back, in part, to the influence of the pantheistic philosophy of India; while the other facet of this theory came about through the influence of the philosophy of Alexandrian Judaism.

[28] Schmithals, *op. cit.*, pp. 183, 184; Bultmann, *Theol.*, Vol. I, p. 182 concludes in his discussion of the gnostic concept of liberty, ". . . the consequence will either be asceticism, which strives either to demonstrate or anxiously to preserve the 'pneumatic' quality of the liberty, or it will be libertinism, which either strives to demonstrate 'liberty' or uses it as a pretext."

[29] van den Bergh van Eysinga, *ZNTW*, XIII (1912), p. 303.

Chapter Four

[1] Newman, *op. cit.*, p. 135.

[2] On the Nicolaitans, cf. Adolf Von Harnack, "The Sect of the Nicolaitans and Nicolaus, the Deacon in Jerusalem," *The Journal of Religion*, III (1923), pp. 413-422, who concludes that the sect of Nicolaitans, known through the writings of Irenaeus, Hippolytus, Clement of Alexandria, and others, claimed a relationship to Nicolaus, the deacon of Jerusalem (Acts 6:5), but with no justification. On the other hand, it is possible that the author of Revelation used the name symbolically as a rough etymological equivalent of the Hebrew *Balaam*, meaning "he has consumed a people." Still I. T. Beckwith, *op. cit.*, p. 460, affirms that a purely symbolical interpretation of the name based upon a supposed identity of these Greek and Hebrew terms is "not supported by certain etymology and is too artificial." However, if the name is not used in Revelation as symbolic, then it is the only one of three (Balaam, Jezebel) that is not used symbolically.

On the basis of Harnack's study the following summary may be made of the Nicolaitans. They were gnostics with a dualistic theology, perhaps of Persian origin, for the basis of their ethics. Connected with their philosophy was a "well-developed speculative philosophy of aeons." They were a sect who had entered the churches of Asia Minor through false prophets and teachers, declaring that faith in Christ and baptism were essential, and teaching that the resurrection had taken place at baptism. They are known to have existed until about A.D. 200.

[3] Both in later Judaism and in the New Testament, Balaam is the father and leader of all false teachings, of libertinism, and of those who despise angels. Cf. the discussion of George Kuhn, "Balaam," *Theologisches Wörterbuch zum Neuen Testament* (Th. Wb.), ed. Gerhard Kittel (Stuttgart: Verlag von W. Kohlhammer, 1952), Vol. I, p. 521.

[4] On Jezebel, cf. Hugo Odeberg, "Jezebel," *Th. Wb.*, Vol. III, p. 218.

[5] There is insufficient evidence to conclude any loss of property due to political persecution (Beckwith, *op. cit.*, p. 453); and the reference to the charge of blasphemy indicates that there was no persecution present at the time (Lohmeyer, *Comm.*, p. 24).

[6] Charles, *Comm.*, Vol. I, p. 58; Beckwith, *op. cit.*, p. 454.

[7] Lohmeyer, *Comm.*, p. 24 suggests the former alternative; Beckwith, *op. cit.*, pp. 468, 469; Bousset, *op. cit.*, p. 220, and Charles, *Comm.*, Vol. I, pp. 73, 74 pursue the latter view.

[8] Lohmeyer, *Comm.*, p. 25.

[9] The text is furnished by Lohmeyer, *Comm.*, p. 204.

[10] *Evangelium Veritatis*, XXII^r, pp. 19-24, Malinine, Puech, Quispel, eds. (Zurich: Rascher Verlag, 1956), p. 111.

[11] Cf. Bousset, *op. cit.*, p. 243.

[12] Charles, *Comm.*, Vol. I, p. 110.

[13] Lohmeyer, *Comm.*, p. 43.

[14] Charles, *Comm.*, Vol. I, p. 20.

[15] The reader is directed to the commentaries *in loc.* and to the following articles: Gunther Bornkamm, "Die Komposition der Apokalyptischen Visionen in der Offenbarung Johannis," *ZNTW*, XXXVI (1937), 132-149; F. Dornseiff, "Die Apokalyptischen Reiter," *ibid.*, XXXVIII (1939), 196-197; Otto Roller, "Das Buch mit Sieben Siegeln," *ibid.*, XXXVI (1937), 98-112; W. Sattler, "Das Buch mit Sieben Siegeln. II Die Bücher der Werke und das Buch des Lebens," *ibid.*, XXI (1922), 43-53; Karl Staritz, "Zu Offenbarung Johannis 5:1," *ibid.*, XXX (1931), 157-170; Müller, "Die Apokalyptischen Reiter," *ibid.*, VIII (1907), 290-316; W. S. Taylor, "The Seven Seals in the Revelation of John," *JTS*, XXXI (1930), 266-271. Cf. also Lucetta Mowry, "Revelation 4 — 5 and Early Liturgical Usage," *JBL*, LXXI (1952), 75-84; Otto Piper, "The Apocalypse of John and the Liturgy of the Ancient Church," *Church History*, XX (1951), 10-22.

[16] Cf. Lohmeyer's excellent discussion of the form of Revelation, *Comm.*, pp. 185-89.

[17] Beckwith, *op. cit.*, p. 539.

[18] Carrington, *op. cit.*, p. 210.

[19] Cf. Lohmeyer, *Comm.*, pp. 104 ff.

[20] Cf., for example, Beckwith, *op. cit.*, p. 642, whose approach is representative of that which is most often followed.

[21] van den Bergh van Eysinga, *ZNTW*, XIII, p. 294.

[22] Stephen F. Caiger, *Archaeology and the New Testament* (second edition; London: Cassel and Company Ltd., 1948), p. 150 and van den Bergh van Eysinga, *ZNTW*, XIII, p. 296.

[23] Cf. Lohmeyer, *Comm.*, p. 119.

[24] Carrington, *op. cit.*, p. 233, believes thereby that this identifies

the heretics as belonging to the Cainites, who are but an offshoot of the Ophites.

[25] *Ibid.*, p. 237.

[26] *Gospel of Thomas* [28] (86:17-20) in Robert M. Grant and David Noel Freedman, *The Secret Sayings of Jesus* (New York: Doubleday & Company, Inc., 1960), p. 147.

[27] Lohmeyer, *Comm.*, pp. 145-147.

[28] *Ibid.*, p. 145.

[29] *Ibid.*, p. 155.

Chapter Five

[1] Schmithals, *op. cit.*, pp. 255, 256. Cf. p. 249.

[2] Hermann Schammberger, *Die Einheitlichkeit des Jakobusbriefes im antignostischen Kampf* (Gotha: Leipold Klotz, 1936), p. 90.

BIBLIOGRaphy

Books

Bauer, Walter, *Rechtgläubigkeit und Ketzerei im Ältesten Christentum.* Tübingen: Verlag von J. C. B. Mohr (Paul Siebeck), 1934.

Beckwith, I. T., *The Apocalypse of John.* New York: The Macmillan Company, 1919.

Bousset, W., *Die Offenbarung Johannis.* Göttingen: Vandenhoeck und Ruprecht, 1906.

Bultmann, Rudolf, *Primitive Christianity in its Contemporary Setting,* trans. R. H. Fuller. New York: Meridian Books, 1956; and London: Thames and Hudson, Ltd., 1956.

———, *Theology of the New Testament,* 2 vols., trans. Kendrick Gobel. New York: Charles Scribner's Sons, 1951.

Caiger, Stephen F., *Archaeology and the New Testament,* Second edition. London: Cassel and Company, Ltd., 1948.

Carrington, Philip, *The Meaning of the Revelation.* London: Society for the Promotion of Christian Knowledge, 1931.

Charles, R. H., ed. *The Book of Enoch,* Oxford: Clarendon Press, 1893.

——— *The Revelation of St. John, The International Critical*

Commentary, 2 Vols. New York: Charles Scribner's Sons, 1920.

Dodd, C. H., *The Interpretation of the Fourth Gospel.* Cambridge: University Press, 1954.

Enslin, Morton Scott, *Christian Beginnings.* New York: Harper & Row, Publishers, 1938.

Eusebius, *The Ecclesiastical History*, trans. Kirsopp Lake, New York: G. P. Putman's Sons, 1926.

Evangelium Veritatis, Malinine, Peuch, Quispel, editors. Zurich: Rascher Verlag, 1956.

Grant Robert M., and Freedman, David Noel, *The Secret Sayings of Jesus.* New York: Doubleday & Company, Inc., 1960.

Hort, F. J. A., *The First Epistle of St. Peter 1:1 — 2:17.* London: Macmillan, 1898.

Jonas, Hans, *Gnosis und Spätantiker Geist*, 2 vols. Göttingen: Vandenhoeck und Ruprecht, 1934.

Kidd, B. J., *A History of the Church*, 3 vols. Oxford: Clarendon Press, 1922.

Kiddle, Martin, and Ross, M. K., *The Revelation of St. John, The Moffatt New Testament Commentary.* New York: Harper & Row, Publishers, 1940.

Könn, Joseph, *Gott und Satan.* Koln: Benziger Verlag, 1949.

Liesegang, Hans, *Die Gnosis.* Stuttgart: Alfred Krüner Verlag, 1955.

Lietzman, Hans, *The Beginnings of the Christian Church*, Vol. I. of *A History of the Early Church*, trans. Bertram Lee Woolf. Cleveland: Meridian Books, The World Publishing Company, 1953.

Lohmeyer, Ernst, *Die Offenbarung des Johannes*, Band XVI of *Handbuch zum Neuen Testament*, Gunther Bornkamm, ed., Second edition. Tübingen: J. C. B. Mohr (Paul Siebeck), 1953.

Loisy, Alfred, *The Birth of the Christian Religion,* trans. L. P. Jacks. London: George Allen and Unwin, Ltd., 1948.

Mansel, Henry Longueville, *The Gnostic Heresies of the First and Second Centuries.* London: John Murray, 1875.

Moffatt, James, *The General Epistles, The Moffatt New Testament Commentary.* New York: Harper & Row, Publishers, n. d.

———, *Introduction to the Literature of the New Testament.* New York: Charles Scribner's Sons, 1927.

Quispel, Gilles, *Gnosis als Weltreligion.* Zurich: Origo Verlag, 1951.

Ramsay, W. M., *The Letters to the Seven Churches of Asia.* London: Hodder & Stoughton, n.d.

Roberts, Alexander, and Donaldson, James, eds., *The Apostolic Fathers with Justin Martyr and Irenaeus, The Ante-Nicene Fathers.* Grand Rapids: Wm. B. Eerdmans Publishing Co., 1951.

Schammberger, Hermann, *Die Einheitlichkeit des Jacobusbriefes im Antignostischen Kampf.* Gotha: Leipold Klotz. 1936.

Schick, Eduard, *Die Apocalypse. Die Heilige Schrift in Deutscher Ubersetzung, Das Neue Testament,* Karl Staab, ed., Wurzburg: Ecter-Verlag, 1952.

Schmithals, Walter, *Die Gnosis in Kornith, Eine Untersuchung zu den Korintherbriefen.* Göttingen: Vandenhoeck und Ruprecht, 1956.

Schneider, Carl, *Geitesgeschichte des Antiken Christentums,* 2 vols. München: C. H. Beck'sche Verlagsbuchhandlung, 1954.

Schoeps, Hans-Joachim, *Urgemeinde Judenchristentum Gnosis.* Tübingen: J. C. B. Mohr (Paul Siebeck), 1956.

Selwyn, E. G., *The First Epistle of St. Peter.* London: Macmillan and Co., Ltd., 1949.

Walker, Williston, *A History of the Christian Church*. New York: Charles Scribner's Sons, 1950.

Wilson, R. McL., *The Gnostic Problem, A Study of the Relations Between Hellenistic Judaism and the Gnostic Heresy*. London: A. R. Mowbray and Co., 1958.

Windisch, Hans, *Die Katholischen Briefe*, Third edition. Tübingen: Verlag J. C. B. Mohr (Paul Siebeck), 1951.

Wohlenberg, D. G., *Der Erste und Zweite Petrusbrief und der Judasbrief*. Leipzig: A. Diechert'sche Verlagsbuchhandlung Werner Scholl, 1915.

Zahn, Theodor, *Die Offenbarung des Johannes*, Third edition. Leipzig: A. Deichert'sche Verlagsbuchhandlung Dr. Werner Scholl, 1924.

Articles

Bornkamm, Gunther, "Die Komposition der Apokalyptischen Visionen in der Offenbarung Johannis," *Zeitschrift für Neutestamentliche Wissenschaft*, XXXVI (1937), pp. 139-149.

Dornseiff, F., "Die Apokalyptischen Reiter," *Zeitschrift für Neutestamentliche Wissenschaft*, XXXVIII (1939), pp. 196-197.

Ignatius, "Ephesians," *Early Christian Fathers*, ed. Cyril Richardson. Philadelphia: Westminster Press, 1953.

Kuhn, George, "Balaam," Vol. I, *Theologisches Worterbuch zum Neuen Testament*, Gerhard Kittel, ed. Stuttgart: Verlag von W. Kohlhammer 1952, pp. 521 ff.

Lohmeyer, Ernst, "Die Offenbarung des Johannes 1920-1934," *Theologische Rundshau*, VI (1934), pp. 269-314.
———, *ibid.*, VII (1935), pp. 28-62.

Mowry, Lucetta, "Revelation 4 – 5 and Early Liturgical Usage," *Journal of Biblical Literature*, LXXI (1952), pp. 75-84.

Müller, M., "Die Apokalyptischen Reiter," *Zeitschrift für Neutestamentliche Wissenschaft*, VIII (1907), pp. 290-316.

Newman, Barclay, "The Fallacy of the Domitian Hypothesis," *New Testament Studies*, X (October, 1963), pp. 133-139.

Odeberg, Hugo, "Jezebel," Vol. III, *Theologishes Worterbuch zum Neuen Testament*, Gerhard Kittel, ed. Stuttgart: Verlag von W. Kohlhammer, 1952, pp. 218 ff.

Piper, Otto, "The Apocalypse of John and the Liturgy of the Ancient Church," *Church History*, XX (1951), pp. 10-22.

Rist, Martin, "The Revelation of St. John the Divine," Vol. XII of *The Interpreter's Bible*, ed. George Arthur Buttrick. Nashville: Abingdon Press, 1957, pp. 347 ff.

Roller, Otto, "Das Buch mit Sieben Siegeln," *Zeitschrift für Neutestamentliche Wissenschaft*, XXXVI (1937), pp. 98-112.

Sattler, W., "Das Buch mit Sieben Siegeln, II Die Bucher der Werke und das Buch des Lebens," *Zeitschrift für Neutestamentliche Wissenschaft*, XXI (1922), pp. 43-53.

Staritz, Karl, "Zu Offenbarung Johannis 5:1," *Zeitschrift für Neutestamentliche Wissenschaft*, XXX (1931), pp. 157-170.

Taylor, W. S., "The Seven Seals in the Revelation of John," *Journal of Theological Studies*, XXXI (1930), pp. 266-271.

van Eysinga, van den Bergh, "Die in der Apokalypse bekampfte Gnosis," *Zeitschrift für Neutestamentliche Wissenschaft*, XIII (1912), pp. 293-305.

von Harnack, Adolf, "The Sect of the Nicolaitans and Nicolaus, the Deacon in Jerusalem," *The Journal of Religion*, III (1923), pp. 413-422.